WRITING DYNAMICS:
A Guidebook to Written Communications
in the Office of the 80s

Writing Dynamics

A Guidebook to Written Communications in the Office of the 80s

Nancy B. Finn

CBI

CBI Publishing Company, Inc.
51 Sleeper Street
Boston, Massachusetts 02210

Production Editor: Patricia Cronin
Text Designer: Martha White Tenney
Cover Designer: Rogalski Associates
Compositor: Jay's Publishers Services

Finn, Nancy B.
  Writing dynamics.

  1. English language—Rhetoric. 2. English language—Business
  English. I. Title.
PE1408.F46   808'.042   81-12243
ISBN 0-8436-0868-4   AACR2

Printed in the United States of America

Printing (*last digit*): 9 8 7 6 5 4 3 2 1

This book is dedicated
to my husband, Peter,
and my sons, Jeffrey and David,
without whose patience and understanding
this work could not have been accomplished.

Contents

Preface

Four score and seven years ago Our Forefathers brought forth on this continent a new nation, conceived in Liberty and dedicated to the proposition that all men are created equal. (The Writings of Abraham Lincoln Constitutional ed. Vol. VII p. 20)

These famous words of Abraham Lincoln have survived the test of time. Usually such speeches are relegated to archives to collect dust. But this piece of writing is referred to over and over again, not only because President Lincoln was delivering an important message at a critical moment in our history, but because this particular language was written with a poetic elegance and clarity rarely found in official documents.

Not all business communications contain the beauty of script achieved by Mr. Lincoln. However, his use of simple words, short sentences, picture nouns, and action verbs are elements of style that every writer should strive to achieve.

It has been estimated that over 85 percent of all business communications are carried on by means of the written word. A study commission on Federal Paperwork indicated in a report recently that the total cost of generating and storing government communications is somewhere in the range of $100 billion annually. Many additional billions are spent on paperwork in the private sector. Much of this work is unnecessary.

Writing Dynamics: A Guidebook to Written Communications in the Office of the 80s has a two-fold purpose. The first is to serve as a useful guide in the formation and construction of the various business communications utilized by every manager. The second purpose is to question whether or not a particular communication is necessary. The reader will be reminded to think through the purpose of his/her communications. He/she will be asked to evaluate their relevance to the audience to whom they are directed. He/she will be questioned on the necessity of sending the message.

The book will discuss each individual writing format — letters, memos, reports, proposals, oral presentations — in detail. There will be suggestions for developing an effective writing style that is clear, concise, and direct. Correct rules of sentence structure and paragraphing will be emphasized with special attention to word usage and problems of wordiness or "gobbledygook." There will be instructions on the role and importance of editing material and directions on the use of graphics and visuals to help convey a message. Tips suggesting ways to cut down on the glut of paperwork will be offered.

ACKNOWLEDGMENTS

The guidelines suggested in this book are the result of many years of working in the field of corporate public communications. The examples cited are actual samples obtained from various companies and institutions kind enough to offer their assistance. The author wishes to acknowledge those companies that supported this research and allowed samples of their business communications to be analyzed. They include American Universal Insurance Company, Boston Edison, Boston University's Office of Sponsored Program, Dennison Manufacturing Company, Digital Equipment Corporation, Garber Travel, National Hardgoods Distributors Inc., New England Telephone, and the Stop and Shop Companies. Assistance in research for the book was also given by the office of Senator Edward M. Kennedy, which provided materials on governmental communications. The illustrations on pp. 65, 84–87 are used courtesy of the artist, Pamela Harnois, of Garber Travel. The author gratefully acknowledges the help of Crockergraphics of Needham in providing some of the layout examples cited in the book and to Gabrielle A. Brousseau who spent many hours typing the manuscript and checking and proofing the copy.

N.B.F.

WRITING DYNAMICS:
A Guidebook to Written Communications
in the Office of the 80s

1
The Communication Process

The English writer Jonathan Swift once defined good writing as the "art of putting the proper words in the proper places." In business writing today this is almost a forgotten art. The haste of getting the word out, in an era where academic training in basic English skills has been scanty at best, has led to an overabundance of pieces of paper full of verbiage that say little or nothing. An effort must be made to turn this trend around.

SENDER-RECEIVER RELATIONSHIP

Thoughts are expressed in writing for the purpose of communicating, to create a greater understanding of a particular idea or matter. The first step in accomplishing communication is to understand that the act of conveying information involves a sender and a receiver.

Communication takes place any time an individual transfers a thought of his/her own to another person. The sender of the written communication is the writer. The receiver is the reader of the written communication. If the receiver understands the essential message of the sender, communication has occurred.

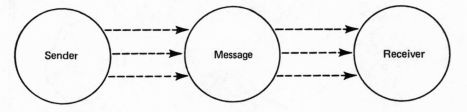

THE AUDIENCE

The sender of a message must also consider the particular characteristics and idiosyncrasies of his/her reader or audience. In other words, the writer must know clearly with whom he/she is in communication. Some of the factors to take into consideration include:

Age
Sex
Occupation
Education
Experience with subject
Position in the business
Attitude toward the subject

The writer should relate the position of the reader to his/her own position. He/she should wonder whether the reader has the background and knowledge to understand the message or whether there is a need to be more explicit.

He/she must determine the importance of including more or less detail: more for the reader who is informed and interested, less for the lackadaisical reader who is likely to neglect to read the entire communication.

The writer should know about the reader's attitude toward the subject under discussion; whether the reader is sympathetic or in opposition to the idea. Every communication must be flavored to appeal to the audience for which it is intended so that it will be read. If it is not read, it is not worth the paper on which it is printed.

THE PURPOSE OF THE MESSAGE

Every message has a purpose. It might be to inform, to influence, to persuade, to educate, to entertain. When setting about to transmit information, a sender must first determine what its purpose is. He/she must ask: Is the message intended to inform about a new policy, product, idea? Is it my intention to influence others using this communication? Am I merely reporting to one group about events that took place among others? Am I trying to educate my readership about a particular issue or idea? Do I wish to persuade someone to come around to my way of thinking via this message that I am about to send? Will my message be more effective if I try to entertain my readers?

Often messages have a multiple purpose. Basically they may just inform, but a bit of persuasion is often thrown in to gain support for the message. For example, the following memo combines elements of information and elements of persuasion.

Interoffice Memo

Memo: To All Employees of Division C
From: Director John Lowe
Re: Research Skills Workshop

A workshop on improving your research skills will be held on four consecutive Mondays, starting next week. All employees from Levels A, B & C are cordially invited to attend free of charge.

Sessions will be held in the cafeteria from 4-6 p.m., and those who wish to participate will be excused from work 30 minutes early.

Although the workshop is optional, all research personnel are urged to attend since the content of the program is directly related to on-the-job performance skills.

The first two paragraphs of the memo merely report the time and place that the workshop will take place. The last paragraph, however, is deliberately included to let the employees know that the workshop is directly relevant to their jobs and that they are "urged" (a strong verb) to be there.

Another memorandum intended to report the agenda of a meeting also contains elements of persuasion for the purpose of garnering support for some of the issues aired at the meeting.

Interoffice Memo

To: All Employees, XYZ Systems Information Inc.
From: Central Office Director, John Lowe
RE: June 8 Administrative Staff Meeting

Key changes in the four major operating divisions of the company were decided upon in a meeting of the Board of Directors today after an extensive review of the budget and the growth potential for the next five years.

These changes include: closing of the operations plant in Minneapolis, and expansion of the manufacturing division in Dahlonega, Tennessee. The Research Division, which operates out of Chattanooga, Tennessee, will be maintained at basically the same size although its budget will be doubled over the next five years. This will require the addition of some key personnel. Central Office, however, will trim its staff by one-third and will compensate for this loss with the purchase of an extensive computer system which will link the company.

We are faced with a troubled economy and the need for our organization to shift from a management-operations-oriented structure to a line organization. All personnel now employed with the company will be retained in some position, although there may have to be several transfers to new locations, especially among those in the Operations Division. This shift will be done with as little disruption as possible to the daily operation of the company and with consideration for the personal needs of individual employees.

Please understand that without these changes, more radical steps would be required in the future in order for the company to maintain its secure financial position.

Additional correspondence, with more detailed explanations, on this matter will be forthcoming.

Note the attempts in the last few paragraphs to explain the reasons for impending plans and changes. The writer is trying to soften the blow of a major reorganization. Note that elements of reporting in the first half of the memo and elements of persuasion combine to make this memo an effective communication tool.

Whatever the purpose of a particular written document, communications constitute an important part of the daily conduct of business. Correspondence is important because there is a belief in every organization that individuals constantly seek new knowledge and current information about what is going on in order to function effectively in job performance. This is the reporting function — the task of keeping information flowing in all directions.

There is also a "Need to Know" factor, genuinely felt, by many department heads, to be the essence of good management. This "Need to Know" translates into a stream of written communications based on the feeling that as long as everyone is fully appraised as to what is happening, harmony will reign. Too often, however, this results in the creation of many useless documents written for the sole purpose of covering one's tracks. As a result, the purpose of the communication becomes obscured and whole groups of individuals become buried in a myriad of words — meaningless pieces of paper, which in fact have no real purpose.

It is important that the writer of a business communication clearly defines the audience in terms of the purpose of the communication and sends that document only to those individuals for whom the communication has meaning. If this were done there would be a great reduction in the number of pieces of mail received by all management personnel, and management time would be used more efficiently.

THE FORMAT

There is another consideration when writing a business communication — the format one is going to use in conveying the message to the reader. Format choices include: letters, memoranda, reports, and proposals. A brief overview of the characteristics of each format reveals that letters are more formal than memoranda. They also tend to be shorter and more direct. Usually letters are used outside the confines of a company, while memos are more commonly used to convey information within an organization.

Memoranda seem to be a catchall for many companies. They can vary from three paragraphs to thirty pages and are still labeled "memos." They are usually written in an informal, breezy style and are typed on a piece of stationery that has been designated in some way as an "INTEROFFICE MEMO." They have a flexibility that allows the writer great freedom in his/her approach to the communication.

The function of the report is to provide an objective account of a particular idea or situation. Reports are longer and require more documentation and evidence of research than the other formats. Generally they must conform to a particular structure or design.

A proposal is a special format designed to introduce a new idea or plan of action. As the report is objective, the proposal is subjective and must sell the writer of the proposal along with the idea being suggested.

Decisions about the purpose of a communication and its format must be made together. As will be evident in later chapters, certain formats lend themselves better to the attainment of certain goals. In summary, there are three major areas of concern for the writer of a business communication which must be determined before any writing takes place:

1. Audience
   Age
   Position
   Attitude
   Experience
2. Purpose
   To Inform
   To Influence
   To Persuade
   To Educate
   To Entertain
3. Format
   Letter
   Memo
   Report
   Proposal

Once these elements are determined, it is time to think about putting the proper words in the proper places. For that the writer needs a strong command of the English language and a basic style suitable to good business communication.

SPOT CHECK ON MESSAGE CONTENT
AND FORMAT

1. Who is the reader of my communication?
2. What is the reader's position and background?
3. What is the purpose of my communication?
4. What am I trying to convey to my reader?
5. On the basis of the answers to the above questions, should my communication take the form of a letter? Memorandum? Report? Proposal?
6. Is my material as interesting and understandable as it can be?
7. Does my communication accomplish its purpose?
8. Am I sending this communication only to those individuals for whom it serves an important purpose?
9. Am I clear on my intentions before I write?
10. Have I answered all of these questions satisfactorily?

2

Straight Grammar

Former Managing Editor of the *New York Times,* Theodore M. Bernstein, regarded by many as an expert on contemporary language, wrote in the introduction of his book "The Careful Writer"

> Writing is one art form that can be practiced almost anywhere, at almost any time. Normally you cannot paint in the office or sculpture in the classroom, or play the piano in a plane or the trumpet on a train. But given some paper and a writing implement, one can write in any of these places. What emerges will not always be a work of art; yet it could be. At the very least we can introduce clarity, precision and grace into the most ordinary of our written communications.
>
> People are accustomed to thinking of their everyday writing efforts — the business letter, the thank-you note, the student history exercise, the news story, the advertisement, the press release, the legal brief — as if they were forms in which one merely filled in the blanks. But they need not be that. There is always scope for originality and adroit phrasing, and always need for logical thinking and clear expression. These things do not usually come spontaneously; they require thought and mental discipline. Thus, unless one belongs to that tiny minority who can speak directly and beautifully, one should not write as one talks. To do so is to indulge in a kind of stenography, not writing.
>
> Naturally, there is no guarantee that the well-written brief will win the suit or that the well-written theme will be graded "A", any more than there is a guarantee that good writing will, by itself, make a novel a best seller. What good writing can do, however, is to assure that the writer is really in communication with the reader, that he is delivering his message unmistakably and, perhaps, excellently. When that happens, the reader takes satisfaction in the reading and the writer takes joy in the writing.

This chapter and the next will deal with the elements that form a communication into the kind of clear, precise writing that Mr. Bernstein is referring to. Recent studies have shown that clearly written communications are hard to find in business today. During the late 1960s and early 1970s, schools and colleges neglected teaching the basic skills in grammar, spelling, punctuation as the wave of open education and free thinking swept the nation. And television's impact, with its visual appeal, took young, growing minds away from the rigours of reading as they sat in passive receptivity in front of the "tube." As a result, those basic skills were never established. Elementary and high school, college, and even graduate school years were completed without even so much as a suitable writing course required.

Today, all that is changing. In the late 1970s a national cry was heard for a return to the basic skills. Congress passed laws paving the way for government grants to be available for the teaching of basic skills training. High schools across the nation changed their graduation requirements so that students had to write frequently and exhibit a certain level of ability before graduating. Colleges have instituted required courses for all freshmen that teach the basic grammar, spelling, and other writing skills they should have learned in the secondary school years.

Businesses, recognizing the need for writing reforms and retraining, have established programs to train not only the secretaries, but also many of the executives how to write clear, meaningful letters, memos and reports. The war has only begun. With the recognition that bad writing costs money, most businesses just now have realized that their employees need to learn to express themselves more clearly, using the written word. Sloppy habits of a lifetime need to be unlearned, for no organization can afford to allow messages marred by errors in grammar to be sent out. Such messages produce a highly undesirable effect upon their recipients and make a mockery out of a company's attempt to put its best foot forward.

Messages that are accurate, attractive and correct make an excellent impression. They draw attention to the fact that the company employs competent personnel who know how to convey their messages and communicate ideas. The business letters, memoranda, reports, proposals and other communications that emanate from an effective manager's department are a concrete record of his/her ability to manage. Sloppy, dull, ineffective communications indicate sloppy, dull, ineffective management.

Not every businessman is or can be expected to write and dictate like a professional communicator. Yet there are "tricks to the trade." A little concentration and effort will develop good skills.

PARTS OF SPEECH AND THEIR ROLE IN THE SENTENCE

Thoughts are expressed in writing to communicate ideas to a reader. Grammar concerns the signals we use to organize the words that fashion those thoughts into meaningful units. For most individuals, English grammar was something taken in junior and senior high school or in college English and quietly endured. But grammar is always important as we speak, write, or discuss ideas and facts. The words that are the mainspring of our language must be used correctly in a message to convey the exact meaning that is intended by the writer.

There are eight parts of speech which are the foundation of the language. They include:

Nouns
Pronouns
Verbs
Adverbs
Prepositions
Adjectives
Conjunctions
Interjections

Nouns

Nouns and verbs are the backbone of the sentence. All other words play a peripheral role in the sentence and, in many cases, can be eliminated. Nouns present no particular problem in business writing. They are the persons, places or things being discussed.

Note this paragraph. All of the nouns are underlined. They are forceful and clear; finding the appropriate noun to use should not be a difficult task for the writer.

> Many electronics corporations are faced today with a serious shortage of trained engineers. This is due to the fact that during the past ten years, schools of engineering graduated far fewer individuals than they had in the past, so that after a slowdown, the need for engineers has greatly increased.

As simple subjects of the sentence, objects of the verb, and objects of the prepositions, nouns present little difficulty. They become a problem in the sentence when they must relate to other words in the sentence; when they must agree with verbs, when they must be changed to pronouns where there is confusion as to agreement between the pronoun and the antecedent. The use of collective nouns and the forming of the possessive of nouns also seems to be an obstacle to some writers.

By keeping to the simple forms of the word and avoiding complex structure, grappling with nouns, pronouns, possessives, singulars, and plurals comes down to a question of the sense of the message you are trying to convey. If the meaning you wish to convey is clear in your mind the choice of noun and the form of the noun you want to use will be evident. Remember to be consistent. If you use a singular noun, use a singular verb and/or a singular form of the pronoun that might refer to the noun. If you use the plural, use the plural throughout.

Verbs

Verbs are the mainstay of written expression. They give action to the sentence. Good verbs add motion, vitality, excitement. Among the major problems in writing that is often confused, unclear and lacking in force is the use of passive verb construction rather than active construction in a sentence. Note the following examples:

Active v. Passive

We *are waiting* for the samples from the marketing department in order to present them during the next meeting.

We *await* the samples to present them at the next meeting.

Profits *were* at an all time high this month.

Profits *hit* an all-time high this month.

Further investigation *is needed* as *is indicated* by current research reports.

Research *indicates* that we need further tests.

Each of the employees *will be given* a copy of the annual report today.

Distribution of the annual report *takes* place today.

A proposal for the reliability assurance tests *is* also in preparation.

We *are preparing* a proposal for reliability assurance tests.

A presentation *was made* to purchasing .

We *made* a presentation to purchasing.

Our reorganization plans *have* not *been* fully *developed* as yet

We *have* not yet *developed* our reorganization plans.

Note that each of the passive sentences uses a form of the verb "to be." They are lacking in force and usually require the use of extra and unnecessary words. The changed sentence in the active form has a clarity and forcefulness that was lacking in the passive construction. It eliminated long prepositional and participial phrases. The sentences have punch and make their point with no hesitation.

Another common problem in using verbs is that writers constantly change the tense (time frame) of their verbs in a particular communication. That is to say that they wander from the past to the present to the future without regard for continuity of thought. The verb tense, once chosen by a writer should remain constant. For example don't say:

Mr. Jones *says* that he *contributed* to the fund.

It should be:

Mr. Jones *said* that he *contributed* to the fund.

or

Mr. Jones *says* that he *contributes* to the fund.

Faulty

It *is* Mr. Hyatt's decision that the contract *was* awarded to us.

Correct

It *is* Mr. Hyatt's decision that the contract *be* awarded to us.

Faulty

Every one of the examiners *reported* that the statement of assets and liabilities *reveals* a good cash position.

Correct

Every one of the examiners *reports* that the statement of assets and liabilities *reveals* a good cash position.

Adjectives and Adverbs

Adjectives and adverbs add interest, vitality, a sparkle to writing that would otherwise be dull and boring. They are the words that give color to your copy with their descriptive detail and explanations of who, when, where. Color is that element in writing that paints a picture in the mind's eye of the reader. Good nouns and active verbs cannot give color to written materials without an assist from good adjectives and adverbs. The following sentence, taken from a company report, is a good example of how a sentence devoid of adjectives and adverbs would be dull, indeed.

The XYZ Company's open office system is the way to reduce the cost of doing business.

change to

The XYZ Company's open office system is the *attractive, practical* way to *substantially* reduce the cost of doing business.

Not only vitality and interest, but clarity is achieved with the use of these descriptive words.

On the other hand, surveys have shown that many of the adjectives in written communications can be removed without any harm done to the message. Indeed, the message is often improved, since these adjectives merely belabor the obvious.

For example:

wealthy millionaire
hard cement
round wheel
liquid oil
brand new product
far fewer opportunities
wet rain
cold snow
etc.

Realistically, there are few business executives who are going to take the time and effort to review the principles of English grammar in order to bring themselves to the point where they have a complete and total mastery of the language. However, they need not go to these extremes. With a basic understanding of the most elemental principles of grammar and a few "hints" about usage, written communications can be greatly enhanced. Awareness of the following items is certain to provide that basis:

1. The question of agreement between nouns, pronouns, and their antecedents
2. The question of using the active voice when writing sentences
3. The question of watching verb tense so that it is constant
4. The question of how many descriptive words are really necessary in a particular sentence to convey a complete message

Only if you are familiar with the grammatical resources of the language can you be in a position to select the most effective way of expressing your meanings. Subsequent chapters will talk about those elements of your style that are necessary to good business communication. With these elements in mind and understanding of the grammatical foundation upon which the language is built, your power of communication will increase. You will then be able to make the choices about sentence structure and word alternatives that you need to enhance your personal effectiveness as a communicator.

SPOT CHECK ON GRAMMAR

1. Am I aware that I may have deficiencies in English grammar? The first step to improved writing is to realize that my writing might need some help.
2. Do I know how to use nouns for the maximum effect? Do I understand how to substitute nouns with pronouns to give my writing variety without having to grapple with improper construction?
3. Have I checked my copy to be sure that all the sentences that can be, are in the active voice; that all my verbs are in the same tense; that I have chosen the most effective verbs I can find for the message I wish to convey?
4. Have I used too many or too few descriptive words to relay my message? Are my choices of adjectives and adverbs appropriate?

3

Elements of an Appropriate Style

The bottom line in communication is clarity. Clarity is conveying the message so that the meaning is without question. Clear writing is evidence of clear thinking. Clear thinking indicates competence. Competence breeds confidence in your business practice.

Proper English grammar provides the tools that will give clarity to your writing. Use of appropriate nouns, active verbs, and only those adjectives and adverbs that add meaning to the sentence, will result in clear, uncluttered communications. These communications are direct. They are simple. No one has difficulty in figuring out just what is the meaning. The following memo, for example, is a good memo. It is direct; it says what it has to say and then stops. The reader does not have to wind his/her way through a multitude of words before he/she learns who, what, where, when, and how.

> There will be a brief meeting on Thursday, June 5, for each division to complete the Company's new Personnel Management Information Form.
>
> Information Services will meet at 8:30 A.M.; Creative Services will meet at 9:00 A.M.; and Energy Development will meet at 9:30 A.M. Attendance is required. Promptness is appreciated.

CLEAR, CRISP COPY

Clear writing avoids long complex explanations when simple ones will do. Clear writing avoids the use of long words when simple one-syllable words are better. Clear writing uses concrete terms, not abstractions that need definitions to make them understandable.

Here is an example taken from the personnel guidelines of a large, well-known corporation. The writing is verbose, cluttered and totally lacking in clarity.

> If special circumstances on an individual situation are deemed necessary to require a variance from the limits established in these guidelines, the case for such a variance shall be presented in writing for review by a committee to be composed of more than five persons who include . . .

The statements, simply and clearly stated might read:

> In circumstances when special consideration is necessary, a request for this review should be submitted in writing to . . .

In all business writing, you must seek out the redundancies, search for repetitive phrases and words, and eliminate them. Long complex explanations should be avoided when simple ones will do. Each sentence should develop the one that came before it. When sentences do not add anything, they should be eliminated.

The copy must be *crisp*! The rule of thumb is to keep sentences short: *15 — 20 words.* Those words should be *75 percent* one-syllable words.

Look at this one sentence from a memorandum sent by a key officer in a large technology firm to several members of his staff. Technical expertise will not help the readers of this memo figure out what in the world the writer is trying to say . . .

Technology Group Charter Issue

Since this group was originally found to provide device technology and reliability support, it was found to be necessary in spending some extra effort to work out some concepts and actions in order to separate and distinguish between the components group and technology group. (44 words)

Phrases such as "it was found," "in spending some extra effort," "in order to separate and distinguish between . . ." result in confused copy that lacks clarity and the crispness that makes the memo a pleasure instead of a chore to read. This particular sentence could have been written as follows without leaving out any of the essential thoughts:

The Technology Group was formed to provide device technology and reliability support. Some time has been spent determining the functions that separate it from the Components Group.

Breaking the longer sentence into two simple sentences lends clarity to the message and eliminates the verbosity found in the original piece of writing.

This memorandum goes on to say:

A meeting which took place *at* (should be, "in") Boylston was fruitful in getting some agreements about these concepts. This will be followed by some action items which are expected to be completed during May, to define the mechanics and mechanisms for interactions and interfacings between the two groups.

"Action items" are abstract, meaningless terms. The use of "mechanics and mechanisms; interactions and interfacings" are verbose and redundant. What is the difference between mechanic and mechanisms? What are interactions and interfacings? The sentence does not really tell us what the findings of the meeting *in* Boylston really were. It is a vague, ambiguous statement that does not communicate.

In that same memo was the sentence:

> With the addition of an additional Quality Engineering Manager, our Management Team will be completed.

The "addition of an additional" is a redundancy. "Quality Engineering Manager" and "Management Team" should not be capitalized. The memo also contained such commonly used phrases as:

> In preparation — a proposal for the reliability assurance tests is also *in preparation.*

> *change to*

> We are preparing a proposal . . .

> The mechanics of interfacing between technology and component groups *are presently being worked* out *in order to present* during the next meeting . . .

> *change to*

> We will present a proposal for interface between technology and component groups at the next meeting.

WATCH THE REDUNDANCIES!

The previous examples illustrate that concise writing that has clarity and crispness does not repeat words or ideas unnecessarily. It also avoids words with overlapping meanings such as:

> absolutely complete
> advance planning
> ask the question
> assembled together
> four last pages

kind of a person
most everyone
real angry
heard where
all of the men
smallest of the two
maybe delayed
will you be so kind as to please

and avoids such wordy prepositional phrases as:

Wrong	Right
Due to the fact that	Because
In order to	To
As of this date	Today
At the present time	Now, currently
In view of	Because
With regard for	Regarding
Owing to the fact that	Because
Along the lines of	Similar to
In spite of	Although
For the purpose of	For
In a most careful manner	Carefully
In accordance with	By
In as much as	Since, as
Among us four	Among
At a later date	Later
Until such times as	Until
In the event that	If
In reference to	About

USING THE RIGHT WORD

The choice of words is a lifetime study. Skilled writers are always comparing words and how certain words affect people. There is a tendency in business writing to produce correspondence that sounds impressive but that merely shows the writer has a dictionary on his/her desk. This trend has been referred to as "bureaucrates," "legalese" or "gobbledygook." It is the result of an effort by educated individuals to randomly add to their writing long and impressive-sounding words that add little or nothing to the meaning of the message being communicated. These words give the appearance of being major pronouncements. They seem to make the writer appear knowledgeable while he/she is actually saying little.

"Gobbledygook" is a skill. Like ice skating, once learned, it is never forgotten. Business and government documents tend, too often, to rely on long, multi-syllabic words, which add little meaning to the message. Let us illustrate this by playing the following word game.

The procedure for the game is simple. There are three columns of "buzzwords," each column is numbered from 1–9. Using any three digit number, taking one from each column, impressive-sounding phrases can be picked out and dropped into any report or memo to give it a ring of authority. No one will understand what the writer is talking about, and no one will admit it either.

Column One	Column Two	Column Three
1. Relevant	1. Transitional	1. Response
2. Total	2. Existential	2. Commitment
3. Integrated	3. Reciprocal	3. Options
4. Parallel	4. Digital	4. Projection
5. Fulfilling	5. Systematized	5. Contingency
6. Compatible	6. Experimental	6. Crisis
7. Authentic	7. Implemental	7. Communications
8. Functional	8. Incremental	8. Identity
9. Synchronized	9. Management	9. Dialogue

Take Numbers 1,6,5: "Relevant Experimental Contingency" or 6,3,9," Compatible Reciprocal Dialogue." Impressive sounding? Sure they are, and dropped casually into your average business memo or report they sound like you certainly know what you are talking about. But do they succeed in their mission of truly communicating the message? Do phrases such as these say something important without wasting the time of the reader?

Admittedly, in all business writing a certain amount of jargon is necessary. Each profession, each trade, each interest from medicine to chess playing, has a language or a number of words which are identified with that interest or profession and commonly recognized by its members. Even the most skilled of writers would not claim that it would be feasible or even desirable to eliminate all jargon from writing. However, when jargon becomes the predominant element in a particular piece of writing, and is used in combination with those "buzz" words we described in the word game, the message too often becomes garbled and pompous. It then fails to communicate. Notice in the following memorandum how these overly long sentences incorporate not only trade jargon, but "buzz word" phrases and verbosity to produce a message that has little meaning to the store managers to whom it was sent:

To: All Store Managers
From: Edward Ward
Subject: General Comments Re: Inventory Requests

We are now dealing with an *expanded procedure* and added *work-load burden* at *store level whereby* we are now requesting special inventories on a large portion of all advertised items — on top of the regular inventory schedules the stores are doing.

Reference to the most recent inventory strips filed seems to be *procedurally difficult* and, in some cases, impossible to accumulate all the individual store inventories from the strip history and to find inventories current enough to be used as the basis to make *ordering decisions.*

Not only are these sentences filled with jargon and buzz phrases but they are grammatically incorrect, combining too many elements into one sentence and making it very difficult for the reader to understand.

Rewritten this might read:

The general office would like all stores to expand their inventory records starting next week. Although we realize that it means an added task for each store manager, we feel it is necessary to have special inventories of all advertised items in addition to the regular inventory schedules you have been doing in the past.

This new policy was decided upon after a review of our inventory strips revealed that we did not have enough information, using the present procedure, to make sound ordering decisions.

Note that the rewritten memo is not only clearer but is more personal and provides a more explicit explanation, which should certainly lead to a better acceptance of the policy change.

Complete writing means that nothing is left out, that no important thought or matter has been neglected. Completeness is not, however, synonymous with wordiness. Good writing is concise. Concise means that no more words than necessary have been used to impart the meaning the writer intends to convey. One way to accomplish this is to watch out for passive construction and to change those sentences to active ones. Another way is to eliminate those words with overlapping meanings, or prepositional phrases that serve no useful function in the sentence.

Many years ago Boston Globe syndicated columnist Jack Thomas wrote in an article entitled: *"There's A Word of Difference"*

> Ignore anyone who says that words are not important. Why should we be satisfied to convey or to receive only the general drift in speech or writing? Why should we be satisfied with anything less than the highest standard both in our choice of precise words and in their careful, orderly arrangement?
>
> If we do not attend to the words we say and write and to the words we hear and read, the alternative is obscurity, incoherence, jargon, illiteracy, boredom and overlong, dull, misleading prose that will lead eventually to muddled thinking.

In business we cannot afford to have muddled thinking!

SPOT CHECK ON STYLE

1. Is my writing clear, direct?
2. Do my sentences pass the crispness test: 15 words per sentence; 75 percent one syllable words?
3. Have I repeated myself unnecessarily by using repetitive phrases or the same word several times within a sentence or paragraph?
4. Am I deliberately packing my sentences with long but meaningless "buzz words?"
5. Have I limited my use of professional jargon to only those words which would convey my meaning forcefully, or have I loaded my sentences with professional gobbledygook?
6. Have I sacrificed clarity for "gobbledygook" in an effort to be clever?

4
Sentence Structure

"You become a good writer just as you become a good joiner, by planing down your sentences." (Anatole France)

Ever try to do the household carpentry chores with rusty nails, a bent screw-driver, a badly worn down hammer? Without the proper tools the job cannot be done. Writing sentences requires those same cleanly polished, well-sharpened tools.

The tools are the words. They combine to make sentences that are properly mitered so that the corners fit smoothly together. All of the elements of grammatical structure now become apparent as you sit down to construct the sentences that will mold your memorandum or report into an effective communication vehicle.

In business writing, the sentence that conveys a thought with economy, precision, and regard for the reader's interest, is a good sentence. Writing this is a difficult task.

There are some basic rules for constructing good sentences:

ONLY ONE THOUGHT

A sentence must express *one* thought and only *one* thought.

> Inflationary pressures and the rising costs of fuel and food influenced the discussions at the meetings and the resultant information has given the XYZ Company an assessment of what is concerning our customers at the end of the 70s.

This sentence contains nearly forty words and seems to have two basic ideas:

1. That inflation and the rising cost of fuel was a factor at a particular series of meetings
2. That the information gleaned from the discussions at the meetings gave the XYZ Company input about customer concerns during the 1970s

The sentence is too long and contains too many elements. It should be re-written to say:

> The meetings focused on the problems of inflationary pressures and the rising costs of fuel and food. These discussions and the information presented have given the XYZ Company a closer assessment of what is concerning customers at the end of the 1970s.

Here's another sentence — it seems that this one does not even contain a single, intelligible thought:

> Started three years ago by a Midwest company, Industrial Services Inc., the promoters believe it is the first time a non-employment agency has put so many companies and potential employees under one floor for matchmaking purposes.

This forty-word sentence seems to pack in so many ideas that the result is a jumble of thoughts that make no sense at all.

When you are having trouble with a sentence, try writing out all the ideas in separate simple sentences. Then you might be able to combine some of the elements you wish to discuss into a unified sensible message.

NO SYNTAX SINS

The syntax or arrangement of words in the sentence should be grammatically correct. In other words, the sentence must have a subject and a verb or it is not a sentence but a mere fragment. It must have the proper punctuation, capitalization, and word order.

> A noted speaker on the subject of the women's movement and with extensive experience in legislative action involving equal rights and other political matters . . .

This sentence is a fragment. It contains no verb and chatters on aimlessly.

Syntax errors also occur with the fused or run-on sentence that serves only to confuse the reader and to neglect the basic precepts of good clear English:

> Reflecting on the continued strength in employment New England's seasonally adjusted unemployment rate declined to 5.2 percent in February from 5.6 percent in January and in February, 1979, while the jobless rate also declined in the other New England States.

Whatever this sentence is trying to say it is not obvious from the words put together here. It would be a lot clearer to state:

> New England continues to experience lower unemployment with a 5.2 percent unemployment rate in February. This is lower than the January figure and in line with the other New England States.

The corrected sentence also eliminates the "dangling" participial phrase "Reflecting on the continued strength . . ." and opens with a strong statement of fact. Dangling phrases in the sentence are a common problem in writing. They are phrases that do not clearly and logically refer to the appropriate noun or pronoun. Here are some other examples of danglers:

> Reviewing the report, a number of errors in computation were found.

> Resuming production today the employees signed the contract.

> Returning from the national sales conference on Tuesday, several excellent promotional plans were revealed by the Director.

Errors of syntax include the use of fragments, run-on sentences, and the placement of improper "danglers," all of which confuse the reader.

SAY WHAT YOU MEAN –
DIRECT, CLEAR SENTENCES

Sentences that are vague, that use abstract terms and extra phrases, are weak and ineffective. To have coherence in writing, sentences must be specific. They must be razor sharp in their meaning so that there is no doubt or misunderstanding as to the intent of the writer. Note how the following sentences are verbose, and loaded with clichés. Rewritten, they are stronger and more forceful.

> *Faulty*
> We are sending you quotations *on the castings about which you inquired* thus *clearing the way for you to* complete your bid.

> *Improved*
> Here are the casting prices so that you may complete your bid.

> *Faulty*
> The product is a stable line of goods, *so it is not subject, except in minor details,* to fluctuations in taste or fashion.

> *Improved*
> This product is stable and its price will not fluctuate.

PARALLEL LINES . . .

There are many stylistic and grammatical devices to improve the communication process. One that is most useful is parallel construction. This is the writing of complex sentences using word choices that are similar in grammatical construction. Parallelism is a good way to organize writing, to keep simplicity and directness in copy, to achieve clarity.

> *Faulty*
> *After reviewing* the report, a number of errors *were discovered* by Mr. Hart.

> *Improved*
> Mr. Hart *reviewed* the report and *found* a number of errors.

> *Faulty*
> We are constantly *adding* new patterns to our line to *prevent* our stock from becoming cumbersome, *thus compelling us* to discontinue a number occasionally.

> *Improved*
> We are constantly *adding* new patterns to our line, *preventing* our stock from becoming cumbersome and *compelling* us to occasionally discontinue certain items.

Parallel structure will show that one idea is as valuable as another and will give equal strength to similar ideas. Connective words like "and," "but," "or," "nor," "for," "to," join clause to clause, phrase to phrase, word to word.

Parallel structure should also be used when listing items in a series, otherwise the writing will be choppy.

> *Faulty*
> e.g. The functions of the executive staff will be:
> To call all meetings
> Coordinating the membership's roles and responsibilities
> Determine when it is necessary to call in the full Board
> etc.

> *Improved*
> The function of the executive staff will be:
> To call all the meetings
> To coordinate the membership's . . .
> To determine when it is necessary . . .

Parallel structure is a neat and effective way to use the "wordtools" that make up the sentence. It helps the writer to organize and to achieve clarity. It cannot, however, be used in all circumstances and is not a cure-all for the ills of verbosity. It is merely another device for a better writing style.

PARAGRAPH CONSTRUCTION AND FLUID TRANSITIONS

In all written communications, sentences are structured and molded to form paragraphs. If the sentences are clear and effective, then lucid, readable paragraphs will result. In a piece of communication, each new idea requires a new paragraph. The principal elements in any given paragraph include the following:

1. The opening sentence or lead sentence, which establishes the topic of the paragraph
2. A transition (from one paragraph to another), which links one paragraph to another
3. The body of copy that conveys the idea in a logical and sensible fashion

There are several transitional words designed to aid the writer in bridging sentences and paragraphs. Some examples are:

> However
> But
> Despite
> Meanwhile
> Therefore
> Nevertheless
> Notwithstanding

These words can be helpful as long as they are used sparingly.

To go from one paragraph to the next, the writer needs to be sure that the first sentence in each of the paragraphs has a connective in it — that is, a word that refers to a sentence in the last paragraph.

The proper flow is achieved when such transitions between sentences and between paragraphs are used.

Note how easily thoughts move from one paragraph to another in the following business letter. The transitional words are underlined.

Dear Sir:

You recently wrote to inquire about our security systems — about costs, maintenance contracts, and related matters.

To give you an overall picture of how our equipment works, I'm sending along some literature that has just come from the printer. It's very up-to-date.

However, pricing is an individual matter, since every installation is unique. As you'll see from the literature, we agree with the police and other experts, that no one security system will satisfy everyone's needs. A good system is one which is adapted to you: you shouldn't have to compromise your needs in order to fit what we design.

So, I've asked our representative in your area, Mrs. Peg Collins, to telephone you. She'll be able to answer your questions, so that you can decide for yourself which kind of system is best for you. You'll be hearing from her within the next week.

Sincerely,

Note the smooth easy flow of the words in this letter. The copy is clear and understandable. The paragraphs are properly bridged, one to another.

VARIETY INCREASES THE READER'S INTEREST

For many pages now we have talked about clarity in writing and have emphasized that one way to achieve clarity is to cut down on the number of words used and to eliminate many of the long heavy words that are so common to the businessperson's everyday language. While this is of importance in effective business communications, it is of equal importance to keep business copy as interesting and readable as possible. So while remembering to aim for a sentence of fifteen words with 75 percent of them one-syllable words, it is also important to add a variety of words to your copy so it is alive and interesting. Nothing is more ineffective than drab, deadly copy that lacks color.

There are many ways to add life and vitality to business communications.

The first way is to utilize colorful, interesting adjectives, which add force and impact to your statements. For example note the difference between these two letters when the adjectives are added:

Dear Counselor:

TRAVEL SCHOOL OF AMERICA offers a course of study to prepare candidates for positions within the Travel Industry. As an institution of Occupational Education, the curriculum consists of a combination of instructional and field training programs during which time each student participates as a trainee in an office.

Dear Counselor:

TRAVEL SCHOOL OF AMERICA offers an *intensive* course of study to prepare *qualified* candidates for *entry-level* positions within the

> Travel Industry. As an institution of Occupational Education, the curriculum consists of a combination of *classroom* instruction and a *"hands-on"* field *training* program during which time each student participates as a *travel counselor trainee* in a travel agency office.

There are times when you add color and excitement to copy by adding the appropriate descriptive words. Another way to give your copy variety is to change the structure of the sentence. Change from a simple declarative statement to a mixture of statements and questions. Insert an interjection, exclamation or a command. Juxtaposition of words within a sentence is also a way to gain variety in a business communication. Note the following examples:

Dull
Dear Mr. Jones:
In answer to your request of June 13, we look forward to a lasting relationship between our companies and are therefore forwarding to you our plan of action for this cooperative venture . . .

Improved
Dear Mr. Jones:
To map out a plan of action on your most attractive proposal, let's get together, shall we?

Dull
Dear Mr. Jones:
Thank you for taking the time for you and your staff to meet with us the other day . . .

Improved
Dear Mr. Jones:
You've sold us, you really have! After meeting with your staff the other day we were so favorably impressed that we will go ahead with the plans to . . .

Other ways to add variety to your copy are to use the current slang expressions, cliches, puns, famous quotations that tie-in with your thoughts or comments. These expressions will give a relevance to your copy and link your thoughts to a current concern or issue. They are fine, however, only when used in moderation. Overused cliches and current expressions become trite and make the writer appear foolish. Care must be taken to pepper your message only when and where it is appropriate. Otherwise you will suffer from a very unpleasant overdose of a good thing.

SPOT CHECK ON SENTENCE STRUCTURE

1. Does the sentence contain more than one idea?
2. Does the sentence have a subject and a verb? Is it a fragment or a run-on sentence?
3. Is the proper punctuation, capitalization, and word order in the sentence?
4. Do I have any dangling phrases in the sentence?
5. Is my sentence clear, or have I confused it with a lot of meaningless cliches, verbose expressions?
6. Would my sentence be improved by changing the structure of it to parallel construction?
7. Have I used the proper transitions between my sentences and between my paragraphs? Have I varied my transitions so that I am not always using the same word?
8. Does my writing have variety or is it drab and dull?

5
Editing

All good writing has one thing in common. It has been organized even before a word was put on paper and it was edited after the first rough draft was completed. The editing process is a two-phase operation. It involves the planning and orderly arrangement of thoughts before writing and the careful scanning of sentences and paragraphs after the message has been completed. The job of the writer does not end until a final seal has been placed on the envelope and the manuscript is ready to go into the "Out" box.

Chapter One talked about determining the purpose of your communication, analyzing the audience, and deciding upon the format you will use. After these questions have been answered and the necessary information has been gathered, all written communications must be laid out in an organizational outline, on paper, so that similar ideas are expressed in the same section; so that extra words and ideas are discarded; so that the proper transitions will be used from sentence to sentence and from paragraph to paragraph.

"Writing is rewriting," says noted writing expert Rudolph Flesch. Effective writing comes from rereading what you have written and taking things out that don't belong.

OUTLINE BEFORE FOR
GOOD RESULTS AFTER . . .

Even the shortest memo should be outlined before it is written. Usually with a short memo this "quickie" outline results in a more effective, informative piece of communication that is easily written and does not have to be rewritten.

For longer reports an outline is essential. It should be detailed enough so that the paper can be written from the outline, topic by topic, by merely substituting completed sentences, with their appropriate transitions and notations, for the topic headings. This is possible because when the outline is completed it should answer the following questions:

1. Have I included everything that I need to cover?
2. Are there any redundancies in my topic headings?
3. Are there sections that are not applicable to what I need to say?
4. Do I need further research to cover some of my outline's topics before I start to write?
5. Is my outline properly organized, or do I need to shuffle around some of my ideas so that my final report will make sense?
6. Can I see the proper bridges and transitions between my topic headings?
7. With this outline, am I ready to write?

Work over your outline. Rearrange your ideas at that stage of your writing if you want a well-organized, meaningful message. Make sure you have answered all of the above questions satisfactorily before you go on with your project.

The following report and the outline that preceeded it give you an illustration of what it is like to outline in detail and come up with this final report. The author of this particular report said that it took at least two outline revisions and at least two rough drafts before he was satisfied with the message.

"The Fuel Adjustment Charge"
A Report to Consumers

Outline
 I. General Statement
    A. Purpose of fuel charge.
    B. Impact of oil cost on energy.
    C. Impact of oil increases — dollars, percentages.
    D. Relation of oil increases to inflation.
    E. Explanation of electric bill and relation to fuel.
 II. What is the Fuel Adjustment
    A. History of Fuel inclusion in electric bill.
       1. Prior to W.W. I.
       2. 1974 procedures.
    B. Understanding fuel charge.
       1. That it does not result in profit.
       2. That it had to be approved by DPU.
       3. That it pays only for the fuel needed to make the power.
       4. That Edison is working to reduce dependence on oil.
          a. Conservation statistics.
          b. Pilgrim I savings.
          c. Other ways to get energy.
             (1) Waste, water, wind.
             (2) Introduce efficiency into operation of oil plants.
             (3) Request permission from Fed. Government to burn cheaper oil.
III. The bottom line, i.e., the cost statistics.

THE FUEL ADJUSTMENT
CHARGE

The fuel charge is simply your share of the cost of fuel necessary to make the electricity you use.

In New England, however, two thirds of our electrical energy needs are met by expensive imported oil.

The price of oil went from an average cost of $12.60 in 1978 to a year-end cost in 1979 of $26.15.

That's an increase of about 107 percent.

Yet, during 1979, while your electric bill was going up about 9 percent, inflation was raising prices at 13 percent.

Your total electric bill is divided into two parts. One part represents the electricity you use and the other represents the oil used to make that electricity, much the same way fabric is included in the cost of clothing you buy.

In 1979, the fuel portion of your bill increased more than 20 percent, while the electric portion increased less than 4 percent.

Now, several points have to be made about the fuel adjustment.

☐ Fuel has always been part of your electric bill, but without the fuel adjustment clause, it was part of the regular rates. Provision for fuel adjustment clauses dates back to 1917 (World War I). They were enacted to assure that utilities could meet fuel costs subject to sudden and unpredictable price fluctuations.

☐ In 1974, the way utilities calculated fuel adjustment charges was standardized. And, the fuel charge became a separate notation on the bill. Actually, it makes a lot of sense. It means we're more accountable for the fuel we charge back to customers. Plus, it gives people an incentive to help reduce our dependence on foreign oil.

Here are some key points to know about the fuel charge:

■ Boston Edison does not make a profit on the fuel adjustment; no rate of return is allowed to be earned on fuel expenses.

■ We have to get public approval of it every month from the DPU.

- The fuel adjustment pays ONLY for the fuel used to make electricity, or for power we have to purchase to meet your electric needs.

- We are working to reduce our dependence on oil for making electricity.

Boston Edison used 1.2 million less barrels of oil in 1979 than 1978.

Pilgrim I saved more than 8 million barrels of oil for a savings of $139 million to our customers.

Electricity by oil cost 4.4 cents per kilowatthour to make.

Electricity by nuclear cost 1.9 cents per kilowatthour to make.

We are actively involved in getting energy from waste, water and wind, and are committed to reducing our dependence on foreign oil.

We operate our oil plants more efficiently — last year we moved up ninth as compared to all other utilities in the country. And, we saved close to $30 million last year in oil costs to our customers.

We've also asked the government to let us burn a cheaper form of oil with a higher sulfur content, something we know we can do without harming the environment and still save our customers an additional $75 million a year.

So, what's the bottom line? In 1979 we reduced fuel charges by $200 million or $36 for each and every one of our customers.

The price of a barrel of oil since 1970:

```
$   2.22 – 1970
$   3.86 – 1971
$   3.97 – 1972
$   4.90 – 1973
$ 12.01 – 1974
$ 12.33 – 1975
$ 11.59 – 1976
$ 13.47 – 1977
$ 12.60 – 1978
$ 19.34 – 1979
```

This is an increase of more than 770 percent; we are currently paying $25 a barrel.

Nuclear fuel savings since 1972 when Pilgrim went on line:

$ 1.4 Million – 1972
$ 25.0 Million – 1973
$ 38.9 Million – 1974
$ 47.1 Million – 1975
$ 41.2 Million – 1976
$ 56.4 Million – 1977
$ 78.1 Million – 1978
$ 139.1 Million – 1979

$427.2 million total fuel savings since commercial operation began.

BOSTON EDISON
800 Boylston St., Boston, MA 02199

ON EDITING

Once a rough draft is written, there are certain elements in every message that must be included — they are the *5Ws and the H*. Who, What, Where, When, Why, How. Every rookie news reporter is told that those words are the pass key to the success of his/her stories.

Looking for the *5Ws and the H* is also the way a businessperson must review his/her communications to see that they contain all of the information desired for an accurate and effective message. This is the first job of editing. If you can answer all of those questions quickly, then your message contains all of the important facts that you need. If one of the links is missing, you had better find out where it is and put it in. If the *5Ws and the H* are in your message but are hard to find, then you lack clarity and need to rethink your approach and style.

The following is an extremely clever memo that was sent to all of the employees in this particular company. In the attempt to be clever, the writer did not lose sight of the fact that the *5Ws and the H* must be included.

Inter-Office Correspondence

To: 3rd Floor/Group Sales/Graphics
        Program Planning/and anyone caught
        singing "oh Danny Boy"
From: O'PERATIONS
Date: March 17, 1980
Subject: ST. PATTY'S DAY CHEER!!!!

Top o' the mornin to you!

Sure n' begorrin tis time to celebrate St. Patty's Day!!!!!! You are cordially invited to celebrate the day of the Green with us. Festivities will begin about 5:15 *O'CLOCK* and you must be wearing some GREEN (Irish Eyes accepted) to enter *O'PERATIONS*! Donations are $1.00 to help supply the "spirits" (what would St. Patty's Day be without them!). Any contributions of "goodies" would surely make us want to bless yer wee heart (no corn beef and cabbage, please!). Just bring them with you if possible. Please try to see Janice O'Bernardi with your donation sometime during your lunch minutes.

Who: The Staff
What: A party for St. Patrick's Day
Where: Operations Department
When: 5:15 p.m.
How: Must be wearing some green and bring $1.00

Once you have checked for basic facts, you face the difficult process of editing your copy for clarity. Each sentence must be read and analyzed. Each paragraph checked for the sense of the meaning. Several questions might be asked:

1. Is the sentence a clear statement of what I want to say?
2. Are the transitions from sentence to sentence, paragraph to paragraph reasonable?
3. Are there words in there that could be improved by substituting others which are more directly indicative of what I am trying to say?
4. Have I said it all?

One of the most difficult tasks a writer faces is that of discarding a word that is already in the copy and finding a more suitable substitute. This is what editing is all about. Another task of the editor and one that is equally distressing to most writers is to edit for grammatical errors; errors in spelling, punctuation, syntax. This often involves the use of a dictionary and the recounting of those "horrible" rules of grammar. Anyone writing anything should have a dictionary at his/her side. Its frequent use would be a great help.

When all the obvious editing chores are completed, there remains, for the good writer, the task of determining whether or not the way in which he/she structured the paper is the most effective way. It is in this stage of writing that he/she must determine whether or not he/she should use subheads or subtitles to set off independent units of thought. It is here that he/she must decide whether or not a graphic illustration might be needed to reinforce his/her points.

Editing copy is essential to good communication. Even the most professional and experienced writers know that to write well is to edit well. A careful rereading, with a red pen, of even the simplest memo cannot be passed off too lightly.

Here is a sample rough draft with all of the editing marks that it took to polish this piece of writing into finished copy. This is what all letters, memos and business reports should look like on the first draft. If you are not finding corrections to make, such as appear here, then something is wrong with your approach to your writing.

It ~~has been~~ *is* estimated that over 85 percent of all business communications is ~~carried on~~ *accomplished* by means of the written word. The purpose of this handbook is to serve as a reference for ~~the~~ middle and upper management business ~~professionals~~ *men* who are the generators and recipients of this glut of paperwork.

~~Business/~~*M*anagers are constantly placed in the position of having *to* compose letters to clients, dash off memos to reporting people, *and* issue reports to their supervisors. They are often required to prepare newsletters and bulletins for ~~circulation within~~ *employees of* a division ~~or~~ department. They may be asked to prepare or approve the language for a brochure that will advertise their product.

Several times during the year managers are called upon to give oral presentations on matters ranging from new products to budget reviews.

Words, both oral and written, are the means by which much of the business of the day is conducted. The sale of a product or idea, the promotion of a program or a proposal, all depend upon the uses or abuses of words. ~~for success or failure.~~

This handbook will present the total spectrum of business communications. ~~as they are used today.~~ Each of the writing form*s* ~~which the business professional needs to know~~ will be discussed in depth. This includes the preparation of business letters, memorandum, reports, proposals, newsletters, brochures, and oral presentations.

The handbook will start with a discussion of the purpose of *the* communication. What is the reason for the message? What is the sender-receiver relationship? What is the impact which the sender would like to have upon the receiver? ~~These are some of the questions the handbook will answer.~~

Chapter Two will focus on the principles of good writing style, including a discussion of sentence structure, clarity, word choices, and the organization of the total message. This is the foundation upon which effective business communications rests.

Graphics, visuals, and illustrations have a large role today in ~~the effectiveness of~~ written and oral presentations. The influence of television and billboard advertising results in a public which remembers more from what it has seen than from what it has read. ~~Thus, the handbook will discuss the ways to use graphics and visuals in both the oral and written formats.~~

A final chapter — on business communications and the computer — a look to the future — will deal with a question which, prior to this publication, has not been discussed in any depth before.

There are many occasions when the manager is required not to actually write but to edit and approve a particular written communication. The handbook will include tips on editing and guidelines to follow when evaluating the copy written by others. An appendix at the back of the book will include such reference tools as the editing symbols, appropriate abbreviations and salutations, some basic rules of English grammar and spelling.

The attempt is to make this handbook the most comprehensive available on the bookshelves today so that ~~any effective~~ business manager who has a copy of this book need not look elsewhere for communications guidelines to carry out his/her work in the most efficient and capable manner.

DEP.
~~any~~ on the word any.

SPOT CHECK ON EDITING

1. Have I stopped and taken the time to outline my thoughts before writing so that I will have a communication that combines the best elements of good writing practices?
2. Have I answered the questions, who, what, where, when, why, how in my communication?
3. Have I eliminated all wordiness and jargon in my copy without eliminating any of the essential facts that I need to convey complete accurate information?
4. Is the punctuation appropriate? The spelling accurate? The syntax correct?
5. Can I improve my communication's message and appearance with the use of subheads? Illustrations?

6

Business Letters

"Letters, letters, we get stacks and stacks of letters."

This is a well-known, first line of a song made popular by the Perry Como television show, one of the early shows of the 1950s. Perry is not the only one to receive "stacks and stacks of letters."

Business professionals today are inundated with letters. Studies show that 85 percent of all business communication is carried on by means of the written word. And letters are a large percentage of that figure. The question many should be asking is whether or not the letter you are about to write is necessary. Studies and surveys have indicated that at least 10 percent of all business letters could be totally eliminated; that they serve no useful purpose and that they even have had the reverse impact of producing a negative response on the part of the recipient.

The studies also indicate that 15 percent of the letters written, were composed to clarify previously written letters that were unclear.

The preparation of a letter is costly to a business. It has been estimated that the cost of preparing the average business letter, including the cost of stationery, postage, and labor, is around $5.00 per letter. This figure does not take into account the cost of space for storing all of the correspondence that offices tend to accumulate.

THE PURPOSE OF THE LETTER

The purpose of a business letter is to communicate a short message from one party to another. No one but the writer can determine the importance of the message or whether a simple telephone call might just as easily clear up the matter. And no one but the writer can decide that, perhaps, no comment at all is necessary.

If, however, you decide that a letter is in order; that there is no better way to communicate your concern or problem, there are several factors to keep in mind.

The 18th Century English writer Lord Chesterfield, in a book entitled "LETTERS TO HIS SON," advised:

> The first thing necessary in writing letters of business is extreme clearness . . . every paragraph should be so clear and unambiguous that the dullest fellow in the world may not be able to mistake it, nor obliged to read it twice in order to understand it.

Successful business letters are well organized. They have been outlined before they are written. They embody clarity and conciseness and always take into account that the reader is a busy person who will not wade through a lot of verbiage.

THE TONE OF THE LETTER
KEEP IT POSITIVE!

The tone of your letter should always be positive, not negative. You want to impress your reader with your business competence. You do not want to even suggest any negative thoughts. Generally what concerns the reader most is information that offers benefits to him/her. In other words, the letter must be written with a personal regard and a genuine concern for the reader. For example, in reply to a letter asking about employment opportunities, the following letter so emphasizes the positive that the reader is left with a good feeling about this particular business, even though the letter was a negative one.

Dear Joan,

Thank you for your crisply written note.

Your name will be pulled from the "Active Talent" file whenever we have an assignment. Maybe next week. Maybe next year. We've taken your offer seriously enough to keep you on file.

Sincerely,

Note how different this is from the standard business reply to an employment inquiry that reads something like this:

Dear Joan,

In response to your request for part-time employment, we regret to inform you that we have nothing available at the present time. We will keep your name on file, however, and may contact you sometime in the future.

Thank you for thinking of us.

Sincerely,

Although there is nothing basically wrong with the second reply, it lacks the vitality and the personal warmth of the first note.

There are several negative phrases that seem to crop up frequently in letters. These expressions tend to put the reader immediately on the defensive. A softer approach would certainly get better results.

> **AVOID:**
> Apparently you are not aware
> I do not agree with you
> You failed to
> You claim
> We question
> You do not understand
> We object to
> You led us to believe
> You neglect to
> Your contention
> Your complaint
> Your disregard for
> Your dissatisfaction with
> Your statement was incorrect
> We object to your
> Our records show
> You apparently overlooked
> You are misinformed

The tone of a letter is important because it sets the pace for a relationship that will result from the letter contact. Build goodwill for yourself and your organization by writing in a way that impresses your reader. Be *effective* while not being *affected*. Often it is best to write your letter in the second person "You." That is, to direct the letter personally to your reader. This will capture his attention and create a better impression upon him than an impersonal tone.

Remember that what is appropriate for one reader may not be suitable for another. For example, the use of certain technical words, while excellent for their appropriateness in one instance, may be completely out of line in another. If you are technically oriented, you must be aware of these differences among your readers.

You also need to be careful not to write in a way that might anger or frustrate your reader. At all costs, you should avoid mean and nasty expressions that could offend. For example, don't say:

> I received your most unpleasant letter which complained that I am thirty days late in payment to you . . .

It would be better to phrase your letter:

I have received your letter concerning my delay in payment to you and am forwarding a check which you should receive in the mail . . .

Although it is important to use the "YOU" voice in your letters, this, too, can be overdone. So a balance is needed. Note in these examples that there is a warmth in the second letter that was lacking in the first letter. A mere change of voice and a few words can make a world of difference in the way in which your letter impresses your reader.

Faulty
Dear Mr. Jones,

> *We* have received your request for a review of *our* facilities and *we* regret to inform you that this is not possible at this time.

> *Our* company has a policy of conducting formal tours for visitors and we would be happy to include you in one of these tours. The next one should be scheduled early in the Fall.

> Very truly yours,

Improved
Dear Mr. Jones,

> Your request for a review of XYZ Company's facilities comes a month too early and we are pleased that you are interested in touring our plant.

> We will be conducting tours for persons such as yourself starting in September and will be happy to contact you at that time.

> Very truly yours,

Remember that good customer relations can be made or ruined by your business communications.

Tone is just as important in written communications as is tact in personal relations. Your letters can be abrasive and unpleasant, filled with technical expressions that confuse, or are too patronizing, or your letters can be written with the reader in mind. In writing letters avoid these common mistakes:

1. Don't anger the reader.
2. Don't insult the reader.
3. Don't preach or patronize the reader.
4. Don't argue with your reader.
5. Don't write when *you* are angry.
6. Avoid opinion, sarcasm, humor that might be misunderstood.

THE STYLE OF THE LETTER, KEEP IT CONCISE

Concise writing in business consists of using as few words as possible without sacrificing courtesy and clarity. That is, using as few words as is possible to describe a particular situation and omitting all unnecessary detail. Particularly in a letter, it is important to keep to the essential details and omit all others so that the reader won't become bored and decide not to read the letter at all. Concise writing, however, is writing that does not omit important ideas or facts. As a result, the letter must contain a clear message written as briefly as is possible. The lack of a clear message may result in the need for a letter asking for more information, which requires the writing of another letter clarifying the first two letters. Compound this problem and you can see how much waste there is in the volume of business communications carried on today.

One way to achieve conciseness in your letters is to eliminate the following pompous expressions that commonly appear in many business communications:

Commonly used expression.	Improved concise expression:
We acknowledge receipt of	Thank you for
We are agreeable to your wishes	We like
Please advise us as to	Let us know
As per your letter of	You suggested to
At the present time	Now
Please find enclosed (attached)	Enclosed is
At a later date	Later
We regret to inform you that	We are sorry
With a view to	As a result of
Thank you kindly	Thank you
In receipt of	We received
In order that	So that
Due to the fact that	Because, since
As of this date or to date	Not yet
In compliance with your request	As you requested
I am in receipt of your letter	I received
Prior to	Before
In the near future	Soon

Another way to keep your writing concise is to be sure that your sentences contain only one idea. When you have two ideas you need to convey, separate them into two sentences.

Faulty

We have addressed the problems you mentioned in our meeting and apologize for our poor service record of the past . . .

Improved

We have addressed the problems discussed in our meeting by assigning a new sales representative to your division. We apologize for the inconvenience you experienced.

By breaking the two ideas into two separate sentences, you achieve a clarity and conciseness essential to good business communications. You are also able to say more by completing the first thought.

Paragraphs should also be short in letters: often as short as one sentence. Ideally, paragraphs are less than four lines when typed onto the page.

Faulty

Dear Joe,

This will acknowledge receipt of your letter of November 21, 1979 regarding the basis for calculating Reserve Income. The offer to credit the XYZ Company with Reserve Income was prompted as a counter-offer to our request for a Paid Loss Retrospective Program. As you know, the program's Loss Limitation was increased to $250,000 effective July 1, 1977, and will result in a substantial increase in reserve payments by XYZ Company in future years, hence the reason for the original request in 1978 for a paid Loss Retrospective Program.

Improved

Dear Joe,

We received your letter which asked us for information about the basis for calculating Reserve Income. Let me explain the details.

The offer to credit the XYZ Company with Reserve Income was prompted as a counter-offer to our request for a Paid Loss Retrospective Program. . . . etc

WRITING THE LETTER

Business letters, more than any other communication format, seem to have more grammatical errors in them than is reasonable. Nothing makes a worse impression for a company than a letter that contains misspellings, sentence fragments, and a general use of the language that makes it appear as if the writer is from a foreign tongue.

The following examples were taken from actual letters mailed by their senders to various parties. One would not wonder why they ended up in the circular file and were not even considered seriously.

Dear Sir:

I have been reviewing your company's products and I am interested in obtaining more information on your intire line, with special emphasis on your electronic related goods.

Please send me your cost and retail price list along' with any and all pertinent information.

Thank you for your time and consideration.

Dear Mr Jones

Thank you for calling us to meet with you.

We look forward to servicing your account as professionally and expeditiously ?...

We understand you may want to plan a meeting in Europe for the Fall and we will have our Vice President of Foreign Seminars, Victor Cooper, contact you to help you with your plans.

Thank you again for your time.

Dear Ms. Goode

Your resume has been recieved for review against (?) possible employment opportunities at our company.

I will forward your resume to several of our managers in Research and Development and will let you know if there is any interest.

Thank you for your interest in our company

Note in the above examples the underlined words that are misspelled or misused in the sentence. Note the redundancies and repetitiveness of some of the phraseology. These letters, which are supposed to represent the writer and his/her company, are a poor reflection. They lead the reader to seriously question whether or not he or she would want to work with a company that allows such sloppy work to be sent out.

There are several tips that will make your letters more powerful and meaningful to the reader, above and beyond correct English.

OPENINGS

Most letters begin with the usual salutation, "Dear Mr. or Ms. and a name," followed by a colon. If you know the person well that you are writing to, it is standard business practice today to use first names and a comma.

It is in your first sentence that you make your first and lasting impression. Too many first sentences of letters dwell too long on references to a previous correspondence or a telephone conversation. For example:

> Dear Mr. Jones:
>
> You indicated in your letter of July 3 which I received last week that your company has a new policy which might be of interest to us . .

> Dear Mr. Jones:
>
> It was kind of you to call last Monday and request information about our new engineering system. I am sending you a brochure that, I hope, will explain . . .

These openings are too long and take too much time before they get to the main point of the correspondence. Plunge right into your main point. Don't waste your reader's time and your own time as a writer. The reader already knows what he/she said to you in a previous correspondence or a telephone conversation, so you do not have to remind him. It would be much better to say:

> Dear Mr. Jones,
>
> I find your company's new policy of great interest to us and wish to learn more about it. Please . . .

> or

> Dear Mr. Jones,
>
> Enclosed is a brochure on our new engineering system which you asked about. I hope it will . . .

The subject of your communication must be made clear from the beginning of your opening sentence. Don't get carried away with too many formal introductions and discussions.

CLOSINGS

There are always questions as to which closing is appropriate for your particular communication. There are several common closings which are usually appropriate at any time. They are:

> Sincerely,
> Sincerely yours,
> Truly yours,
> Yours truly,
> Cordially,
> Cordially yours,

Some people like to eliminate the closing completely if the last sentence really ends the message. For example:

> We look forward to hearing from you soon.
> Signature

> Thank you for your time and consideration.
> Signature

> Please let us know if we can be of further assistance.
> Signature

Both an ending sentence and a closing are unnecessary. Keep the closing as short and informal as you can. Make sure that your business letters are hand-signed. Nothing is more offensive than an unsigned or machine-signed letter. Also avoid "cute" closings such as "Hopefully yours." They merely call attention to themselves and detract from the seriousness of your intent.

THE LETTER FORMATS

There are four types of letters that most businesspeople deal with on a frequent basis. They include the sales letters, collection letters, letters of inquiry, and answers to requests and complaints.

Sales Letters

Sales letters have one purpose: to encourage their readers to make a particular purchase. The purpose of the communication is to influence — to influence a person to buy. This may be done by inviting a person into the place of business to make a purchase; by offering an item for sale by mail; or by introducing a sales representative who will personally visit the potential customer.

Writing sales letters takes a certain skill. It involves tact, diplomacy, and the ability to say in just a few words what it might take a salesman/woman hours to explain. Writing the sales letter takes creativity and imagination. Some of the factors for success include:

1. *Plan ahead.* Know to whom you are writing and what his/her needs might be.
2. *Analyze what it is you are trying to sell.* Is the purpose of the letter to sell directly, or to introduce the reader to the product and invite him/her to visit the place of business, or send for further information?
3. *Realize the limitation of the sales letter.* Understand just how short you must keep this letter to be effective. Too many sales letters are filled with extra advertisements and brochures that are sent along with the letter.
4. *Include a personal note with the letter* if it is going to a person with whom you have had contact before. This will often leave the customer with a satisfied, favorable attitude toward your letter. This technique can also be used to attract attention to a special point you wish to make.

The good sales letter must have an appropriate attention-getting opener without being corny and overdone. It must have an extremely positive tone and some creative gimmick to attract the reader and keep him/her from throwing it in the wastebasket. Sales letters have the reputation for being "junk mail," loaded with cliches and weighed down with verbiage. Keep the writing simple. Use an illustration or splash of color on the letter to attract attention. Short slogans are always good openers as are questions or leading statements. In the following example, note that the letter is short but holds your interest.

Sweet Tones Inc

Dear Sir:

If background music was playing in your office or at your job would you work faster? Would you be more efficient or happier with your job?

If the answer to those questions is "yes," you might be interested in our new monthly subscription service "Sweet Tones" Inc.

Sweet Tones will pipe in music to your office or place of business for a low monthly fee, plus the initial installation charge for the required equipment.

If you are interested in our service just fill out the enclosed card, and we will have our local sales representative get in touch with you.

This letter might be printed on a soft blue paper with an appropriate musical design on the letterhead for maximum effectiveness. It is a good sales letter.

Collection Letters

Collection letters are among the most difficult to write because they involve the most tact and diplomacy. With the collection letter, you are trying to procure what is rightfully yours while retaining your reader as a viable and satisfied customer. When the usual billing notice has been ignored by your reader and it is time to take a firmer step, it is the collection letter that you send which will determine your future relationship with the delinquent party. Some tips for success are:

1. Personalize the collection letter. Show that you know your client and understand his/her particular circumstance. Make sure he/she feels that this letter is written directly to him/her and is not a form in which you merely filled in his/her name. For example, note the contrast between the next two examples. The second will get a positive result and a future order while the first will leave ambivalent feelings with the recipient.

> Dear Mr. Jones:
>
> Our records show that your bill is three weeks overdue and we would like to have payment immediately. Please send us your check in the return mail or we will have to turn this account over to our collection attorney.
>
> Sincerely,
>
> Dear Mr. Jones:
>
> If you've already sent in payment for the attached bill we thank you. Our records show that we haven't yet received it. Please let us know if there is a problem that's causing the delay and we will be happy to work out an arrangement. We value you as a customer and would like to continue our mutually satisfactory relationship.
>
> Sincerely,

2. Time your collection notices so that they do not bunch up on your customer. Make sure they are evenly spread over a period of time so they serve as firm reminders of bills overdue without becoming annoying complaints.
3. Try for originality in your collection notices. Often a postcard with a

cartoon indicating that the bill and its payment might have crossed in the mail will have more impact on the customer than another serious reminder. Humor, however, can backfire, so you need to be careful at whom it is directed.

Letters of Inquiry

Letters of inquiry are those that seek information. They are among the most common types of letters that a business finds it necessary to generate. They range from the simple request for a brochure or catalogue to complex letters asking for information, of a research nature, which is not easily available. The business executive may find it necessary to write a letter of inquiry about a potential employee; or a letter inquiring about a new product that might be of interest.

The most important thing to keep in mind when writing a letter of inquiry is to keep it straight and simple. Ask your question and then stop. Don't fill the letter with a lot of extra verbiage that has nothing to do with what you need. For the simple request, all you need to say is:

> Gentlemen:
>
> Please send me your new catalogue #35876 with a price list.
>
> > > Thank you.

or

> Gentlemen:
>
> We are considering the employment of Jim Murphy and understand that he was affiliated with you for the past five years. We would appreciate hearing from you about Jim and his ability to serve as a manager in our local office.
>
> Thank you for your time.

Letters Answering Requests and Complaints

Letters answering requests and complaints, although often considered a nuisance to the business manager, are another important way in which you can present a favorable image for your company. If your answer is cold or lacks clarity, the letter will reflect your uncaring attitude or incompetency. If, however, your letter is well-written, warm, friendly and shows efficiency, it will win the respect of your reader/customer and he or she will remain loyal to your business.

Your objective in answering requests and complaints is to build goodwill for the company and, if possible, influence future sales or new business.

Your success depends upon keeping the following factors in mind:

1. Provide the information requested. Your answer should indicate that you have read the request or complaint carefully and that you understand it. Make sure your answer is thorough and complete and provides the answers sought by the reader.
2. Be brief in your reply. Don't skirt around an issue or engage in a lot of useless discussion. Stick to the point of the letter and include nothing else.
3. Answer promptly. To delay in answering a request or complaint is merely putting off the inevitable and creating a poor image of your company. Why irritate the sender of the request when a prompt reply will create a more favorable impression.
4. Consider a follow-up letter. On some inquiries, and even complaints, a follow-up letter will increase the chances of engaging the inquirer in future business. Keep a file of letters that may require a follow-up and check that file from time to time.
5. Courtesy and friendliness will pay off. Be sure to write your answer in a positive, friendly tone that will win over the inquirer. This, too, is important in retaining that individual for future business.

Note how the following letter incorporates many of these points and provides a satisfactory answer to a touchy situation.

Dear Madam:

Thank you for bringing to our attention the fact that your photo processing order has been misplaced or misdelivered. We realize the value you place on your order, and we are most anxious to locate it for you.

Please fill out the enclosed Tracer Form completely. Any details you can remember about your missing order will be of help to us. We will make every effort to find your film and return it to you as soon as possible. If you should receive your order, please let us know.

We are extremely sorry when incidents such as this occur. Please accept our apology for the delay and inconvenience this has caused.

Sincerely,

SPOT CHECK ON LETTER WRITING

1. Is the letter you are about to write necessary?
2. Have you outlined the concepts of your letter so that it is well organized?
3. When you reread your letter, do you find that it is written in a positive tone?
4. Have you checked your letter for negative phrases and wordy expressions?
5. Is your letter written with your reader in mind? Have you incorporated the "YOU" voice so that the letter is warm and personal?
6. Have you kept the sentences simple and easy to read and your paragraphs short (four lines as a guideline)?
7. Have you checked the letter for grammatical errors, misspellings, correct punctuation marks?
8. Is your opening short and effective?
9. Would your sales letters encourage you to buy or do business with the company?
10. Is your collection letter firm, clear and tactful, or obnoxious in its demand for payment of a bill?
11. On letters of inquiry and answers to requests and complaints do you keep to the subject and present a favorable image for your company?

7
Forms and Formats

In business, first impressions always have counted. The first impression made by your business communication is dependent upon the physical appearance of your communications document. Many businesses have been using the same letterhead for the past 25 years or longer. These old letterheads tend to be dull and weak. They seem to have a similarity of black, block letters that lack distinction. If your business has not redesigned its letterhead recently, it might be time to adopt a new look appropriate to the 1980s. The flavor of the 1980s is bright colors, lots of graphic design, and vitality. New stationery, and the use of logos and symbols to convey a general impression about the business, are necessary.

STATIONERY

There are three items you must consider when thinking about the stationery you wish to use for business correspondence. They are:

1. Color of the paper
2. Paper quality (finish)
3. Size of the paper

In former times, businesses would not even think of using any color but a stark white. Times have changed, and many businesses have very effectively gone to a stationery that is in a muted shade of blue, beige, or oyster. Darker colors are used for the letters. These muted colors are more pleasing to the eye than the traditional white stationery with black letters that glare out of the page.

The finish or stock of the paper used for business correspondence should be of a good quality which allows for easy erasability or adaptability to the correction tape used on the finer electric typewriters.

Although the size of business stationery has traditionally been 8 1/2 by 11, some companies have gone to a somewhat smaller size paper of 7 1/2 by 10 1/2 which is equally sufficient for their needs.

MECHANICS OF LETTER PLACEMENT

The most common format for placing a letter on the page is a picture-frame placement where the side margins are equal and the top and bottom margins are equal, framing the letter into a block-style square that has no indentations.

The parts of the letter include: the letterhead, the date, the inside address, the salutation, the body copy, the close, and the signature. Some letters also contain special instructions or devices, including attention lines, copies made, special mailing instructions, and a postscript. In the 1980s where informality is the rule rather than the exception, there are no musts where letter placement is concerned. The major considerations are neatness and uniformity. Managers would do well to double check and make sure that, in the haste of getting the job done, letters are not sent out with smudges, wrinkles and other marks that would not result in the type of "first impression" that you would desire.

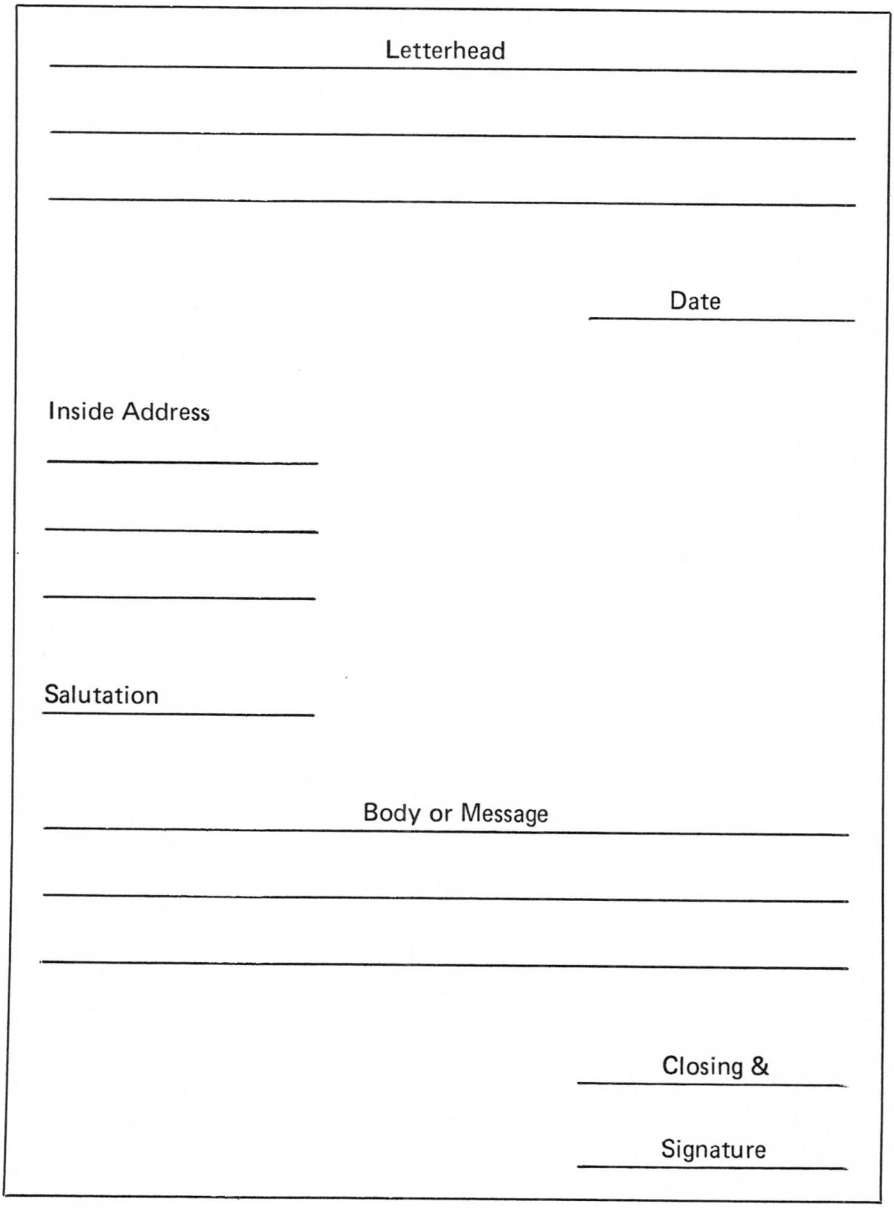

Letterhead

Date

Inside Address

Salutation

Body or Message

Closing &

Signature

There is also a modified block style in which the paragraphs are indented:

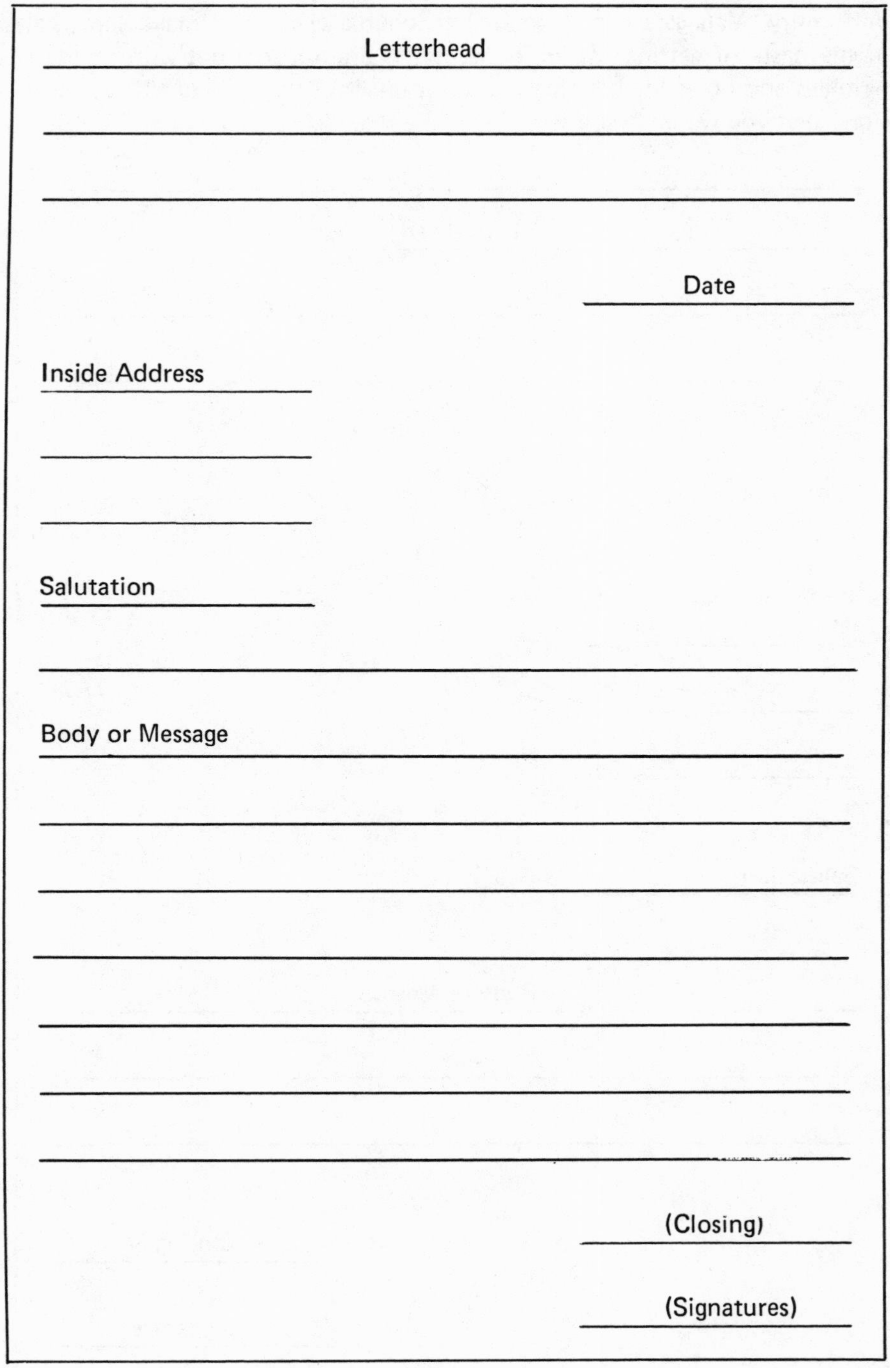

Letterhead
_____

_____

_____

Date
_____

Inside Address
_____

_____

_____

Salutation
_____

_____

Body or Message
_____

_____

_____

_____

_____

_____

(Closing)
_____

(Signatures)
_____

LETTERHEADS

The adoption of a new letterhead involves several considerations. It is important when considering a new "look" to make an initial decision as to the effect you want to create. What is to be the emphasis of your visual message? Is it to be large, small, bright, dull? What is the mood you are trying to create through the visual format you are using? Today, companies are getting away from the traditional black block letters and into a softer look. All sorts of unusual shapes and sizes are being used in letterheads, from script to three-dimensional.

Notice in these examples the contrast between the old "Magic Carpet" and the new. Note the difference in the typeface of the letters used on the flyer. The formerly rigid rule of black block letters only, has given way to all sorts of unusual designs.

Old

New

The second thing you need to consider when redesigning a letterhead or logo is whether or not it captures the attention of your reader. It is the name and the symbol or logo of the organization that a reader will see first. Together they should express the character of the organization. The design must be simple enough to be easily recognized. It must be distinct enough to stand out.

A good idea when thinking about a new letterhead or logo is to rough out a thumbnail sketch of what you are trying to say. When you have refined

We'll be here all summer...

(but **you** don't have to be!)

Old

WE'LL BE HERE
ALL SUMMER...

(BUT YOU DON'T HAVE TO BE!)

New

your ideas and adopted a particular design, you are then ready to seek professional assistance and the preparation of a layout.

FORMS

In an effort to save time, space, and work, many businesses have turned to the use of form letters to cover an abundance of needs. If they are neat and well planned, these form and guide letters can reduce the office work load and the cost of storing voluminous odd pieces of correspondence. However, when abused or not well planned, these form letters can actually be damaging to a business.

Some of the considerations that you should think about when using form letters include:

1. The spacing of items on the letter. Are the individual items placed on the paper so that they lend clarity and easy readability to the form?
2. The size of the print. Is the print used on the form letter large enough and clear enough to be easily read? Too often the person who composes the form letter is trying to squeeze in so much that the letter is not clear.
3. The space for filling-in material. Are the lines for the insertion of answers to questions sufficient for those answers or will they cramp the writer?
4. General attractiveness. Is the print used on the form letter large enough and clear?

A U.S. Government survey taken several years ago indicated that form letters cost up to 90 percent less than individually dictated letters. In this survey, the comparative cost of producing a full-page government letter of approximately 300 words was a minimum of $1.49 for a dictated and typed letter and 9¢ for a printed form letter.

These letters are being used in every situation from the simple sales letter to the acknowledgement of an order. They must be used with relative caution since there is a tendency among businesses to handle too many problems with these hastily conceived, mechanically produced forms. Some of these problems need more personal attention, so the customer will not feel that the company is insensitive to his/her needs.

SPOT CHECK ON DESIGN AND FORMAT

1. Is it time for a new and modern design on the company's communications?
2. How can I get away from the standard white stationery with black, block letters?
3. Is the general appearance of my letters neat and interesting?
4. In creating a new letterhead, do I have a firm idea of the image I want to create in the mind's eye of my reader?
5. Does my letterhead design and/or logo capture the attention of my reader and leave a lasting impression?
6. Could some of my correspondence be effectively consolidated through the use of form letters?
7. Are the form letters I am using effective in their presentation in terms of:
   a. layout on the page
   b. size of the print
   c. spacing of the items
   d. general attractiveness
8. Am I using forms where a letter might be needed to personalize my relationship with certain customers?

8

Writing Memos

"Writers seldom write the things they think. They simply write the things they think other folks think they think."
(Elbert Hubbard)

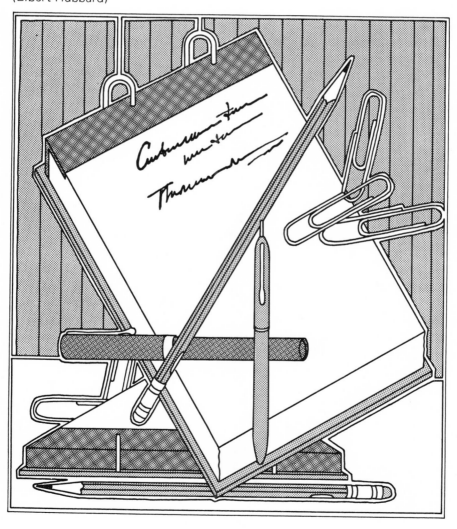

More business communication is carried on through the use of the "INTER-OFFICE MEMO" than through any other means. This format is not only constantly used, it is abused. The purpose of a memo should be to convey a message on a matter of importance from one member of a company or organization to others. The message should contain elements of importance to all who receive it. Memos have become a catchall for all forms of communication. There are short and informal memos and long and involved memos. They can be handwritten or contain several typewritten pages.

One way to avoid sending too many memos is to adhere to the following general rules:

1. If you can convey your message by talking directly to a person, do it. Walk over to the person's office and discuss the matter.
2. If you can't discuss the matter directly, telephone. Using the telephone saves time, money, and cuts down on the overabundance of paperwork now being generated.
3. If none of the above work, then you must write. You must also write a memo if it is to be directed to several individuals. Your time is valuable and you can't be running around to several persons, or sitting on the telephone for an hour repeating the same message.

DETERMINING THE READER

Once you have determined that you must write, it is necessary to define the audience to whom the memo is directed.

Memo writing today can be subtitled: "The Fine Art of Covering Yourself." Too many memos are circulating because managers want to be sure they will never be caught off guard or accused of being negligent. So they dash off a memo to a long list of twenty or more associates in the business to explain anything and everything that can ever be questioned in the future. Sometimes it is necessary to cover yourself. All too often you are merely pushing around papers that result in a blitzkrieg of correspondence that is unnecessary and expensive for the company, which must absorb the cost of supplies, labor, and the storage of all of this paperwork.

According to a report from the Federal Government, the situation is even more acute in the Federal bureaucracy. In this report entitled: "Records and Paperwork Management in the Federal Government: Two Decades of Recommendations," officials reported: "Records and paperwork management are today, as they have been for the past two decades, matters of growing concern and continuous attention." The report goes on to state that, although the matter has been discussed for the past two decades, little or nothing has been done to alleviate the problem. As of the mid-1950s, the report stated, there were more than 25 billion cubic feet of government records in existence, and that the annual cost to the Government of Records Management was approximately four billion dollars.

Much of this problem, both in the Federal Government and in private industry, stems from the glut of memos and reports that a manager feels obligated to send so that he/she will not be criticized at some future date for "failure to communicate."

One major utility has a habit of sending a weekly four to six page memorandum status report to over thirty individuals in the company. Of the thirty, perhaps half have a need to know this information. The others merely receive it out of courtesy or fear.

In summary, it has become imperative today that before writing a memo, managers think about the audience for whom it is intended and what they are trying to accomplish. More care in the selection of recipients would be helpful.

If, in spite of these considerations, you still need to write your memo, the following suggestions might help in making them more readable and more useful as a communication tool.

BASIC MEMO FORMAT

Most memorandum are sent out on pre-printed paper which is labeled:

Office Memorandum
Interoffice Memorandum
Interoffice Communication
MEMO
etc.

Whether it is a long or short memo, serious document, or a "quickie" note, the memo usually includes the following information:

The Date
Your Name
The Name of the Recipient
Names of people who are to receive copies
The Information

Example of a Standard Format:

Office Memorandum

To: John J. Murphy   From: John Doe   Date: August 8, 1980

cc: Dick Evens
    Tom Johnson
    Jean Kramer

Subject: The High School Scholarship Aid Program

It has come to our attention that the company would benefit from establishing a scholarship awards program, and we are seeking individuals who would like to work on this project.

If members of your staff are interested, we are holding a preliminary meeting on Wednesday, September 9, in the Main Cafeteria at the Salisbury headquarters.

Persons interested should contact Tom Johnson as soon as possible so that he can set up a steering committee.

WRITING TIPS

No matter what format your internal office communications take, there are several tips that will help enhance the impression they make and increase their readership.

All interoffice communications must be short and informal. They must be written in a crisp, clear style and must follow the basic principles of writing:

1. One idea to a sentence.
2. No extra words (fifteen per sentence, 75 percent one syllable words).
3. No long verbose expressions that require a dictionary to define them.
4. Whenever possible they should be creative, different, interesting, utilizing attention-getting devices.
5. They should stick to the point and not cover too many different issues.
6. They should adhere to correct English rules and proper sentence structure.
7. They should be written in a positive tone, never negative.

The following are some examples of good and bad memos along with some commentary on each one . . .

Note in the following memo the wordiness, the lack of clarity, the difficulty in reading the copy that is squeezed onto the page. Notice the underlined

---

Interoffice Communication

To: All Employees

Date: March 15, 1980
From: John Jones

For the first time, the companies must report in their Annual State-ments (Schedule T) premiums and losses by state produced on a non-licensed basis. Additionally, some states in which our companies write on a nonlicensed basis will receive or may request what is known as a Page 14, detailing the premiums and losses by class of business for each such individual state.

We can anticipate the states' attempting to match up their Surplus Lines Tax income by company with the data thus supplied them. Ergo, it is imperative we ascertain that the affidavit procedure has been complied with by obtaining a copy of it and the Surplus Lines Tax paid in every case where our brokers are producing risks outside of their own jurisdictions.

It is terribly important that we do this in every instance because it would appear that although our companies technically are not re-sponsible for the payment of the Surplus Lines Tax, we are bound to be involved at least in endless accounting work if our companies must try to reconcile taxes that appear to be unpaid on our business.

---

phrases. The topic for this memo is technical enough but when the English grammar is poor, it makes reading this memo all the more difficult. Avoid using pompous phrases such as "ergo" and "terribly important."

In contrast, note the clarity achieved in the memo below just by the use of the numbered sequence and the short, simple sentences.

Interoffice Memorandum

To: All Buyers
From: Fred Lockwood
Subject: Price Increases
Date: December 13, 1979

Ladies & Gentlemen:

Effective immediately, all price increases are to be submitted to my attention for approval prior to being given to keypunch. The following procedures are to be adhered to:

1. On the master item log, all current costs are to be posted adjacent to the old costs.

2. New suggested costs, in pencil, are to be posted adjacent to the old retails.

3. The buyer must initial the first page of the vendor listing, indicating that he or she has reviewed the work.

4 Submit the books to my office, indicating on an attached memo the vendors involved.

Upon approval, the books will be returned, and the IBM documents can go through the normal channels.

Thank you very much.

The following memorandum, although of a more technical nature, is clear and forceful because of the use of the short lines and paragraphs, and the numbered sequence.

Memorandum

James Maguire   June 21, 1979
Timothy Jones

Burn-Out Date — Assembly Modules

As of May 31, 1978, current EOM inventory is as follows:

Assembly Modules   – 29
Assembly Record books – 61

In addition, our inventory of Modules is as follows:

Assembly Module 1 –   65
Assembly Module 2 –   64
Assembly Module 3 – 106
Assembly Module 4 –   80

Assembly Module 5 - 49
Assembly Module 6 - 54

Burn-out date of complete kits is approximately July 15th.

I recommend that we do the following:

1. Stop sales of all Modules immediately.
   Using the low figure of 49 (Module 5), this will give us enough inventory to take us through August, 1978.
2. Stop selling extra texts, student record books, and text packs immediately.

This will give us additional inventory to take us through April, 1979, taking into consideration that we will have an increased sales force.

USING VISUALS

Among the most difficult memos to write are those that management sends out to its employees. They tend to be stiff, stuffy, formal, and patronizing. They plainly show how awkward the "boss" feels about having to give orders to his/her reporting people. In the following memos, think about how much more effective they could have been if they had a drawing or cartoon to illustrate the points that the management was trying to make.

Inter Office Communication

Co: Date: January 2, 1979
To: The Office Staff   From: Management
Re: Yours:

Members of the Staff have been eating their lunches at their desks. In view of the ever-increasing visits of important outside persons, I am asking you to no longer follow this practice.

We do have a *lounge on the 5th floor* which is intended to be *"UNI-SEX"*! Your cooperation in complying with the above would be most appreciated.

Inter Office Communication

Co: Date: 1/2/79
To: Staff   From: Management
Re: *Dress Code*   Yours:

Even though we do not have a *strict dress code,* we must remind members of our staff that any type of halter tops-jeans-culottes, and clothing of a similar style or nature, are not acceptable for wearing in this office.

Your co-operation in following the above is appreciated.

A sketch such as the following one is also an example of how drawings can often take the place of a wordy memorandum, and with much stronger impact.

Another practice in memo writing, which is to be avoided, is to send out a negative memo or apology such as the following. All of your communications should be in the positive, not in the negative tone.

Memo

To: All Division A Employees
From: Jim Smith, V.P.

We apologize for sending this memo after the fact. However, we inadvertently sent out the staff meeting notices without telling you that each person who attends a staff meeting must make one of the days up.

Originally our plan was that anyone who went on a Friday to Monday meeting would work Tuesday through Saturday of that next week and anyone who went on a Thursday through Sunday meeting would owe us a day and make it up on a schedule which you would send to me. Obviously, the people who have already gone now owe us a day.

This was our policy last time we did four-day staff meetings. Attached is a copy of the London and Acapulco memos.

In view of the fact that we have recently been short-staffed due to Yom Kippur, the Pope's visit, Columbus Day and our staff meetings, we feel that this request is fair.

Faulty

Memo

To: All Division A Employees
From: Jim Smith, V.P.

A bit of clarification . . .

All staff members who attend a staff meeting should plan to make up one of the days. This policy is necessitated by the fact that with all of the recent holidays and the time off for the meetings we have been short-staffed. In fairness to all personnel, this make up day is necessary. It has been our policy in the past as you will note from the attached London and Acapulco memos.

Thank you for cooperating.

Improved

The second memo certainly contains more personal warmth than is evidenced in the short, curt words of the first:

Memo

To: General Personnel
From: Division Headquarters

There will be a Manager's meeting on December 27 at the TSA at 8:45 a.m. to discuss new and simpler bookkeeping procedures which will go into effect on January 2, 1980.

Since this will be a new procedure for the entire Company, it is mandatory that you be there.

Faulty

Memo

To: General Personnel
From: Division Headquarters

All Managers are requested to attend a meeting on December 27 at the TSA at 8:45 a.m. to discuss new and simpler bookkeeping procedures which will go into effect on January 2, 1980.

Since this is a new procedure for the entire Company, we hope this session will provide you with the information for an easy changeover. Plan to see you there.

Improved

In summary, you will note that the success or failure of your memorandum is dependent upon the approach you take in conveying your message to the particular audience you have targeted to receive this communication. Some of the elements to keep in mind include:

1. Keep it short — stick to the main purpose of your communication; once you have finished with that, don't continue your writing.
2. To help achieve clarity in your memos, try to use numbered sequences and subheadlines.
3. Whenever possible try to find a sketch or drawing to illustrate your point in a more interesting way.

4. Never send out a negative memo that, in its attempts to apologize, also tends to be wordy. Use a positive tone without being too cocky.

5. The memo is the most informal of the written business formats — be personal and warm whenever possible.

The following memo illustrates many of these points, — a short, breezy style, eye-catching headline, and warm personal tone.

Systems and Procedures Alert

April 18, 1980
To: Store Managers/Department Managers
From: Larry Walker
Subject: Service Vendor Salesman Check for Wrong Pricing

HOW ABOUT THIS IDEA?

. . . that as a service vendor salesman reviews his program from his preprint (which supposedly has the most current *retail prices*), he checks each item. If stock is low, an order quantity is written — if stock is adequate, pass.

. . . Now suppose that as he checks each item, he verifies that the ticketed price (on the face item) for *each* item on the preprint matches his retail. *If it does not,* he simply puts an "X" beside the item on the preprint.

. . . After he leaves, you will take your copy — find out the correct prices (based on the "X"d items highlighted) and assign someone to reticket the record markup or markdown.

This is not putting an undue burden on the salesman — and will certainly help you spot ticketing errors which must be corrected.

We will be contacting each service vendor factory to arrange that they institute this procedure "officially" with their reps.

In the meanwhile, please speak to each rep — ask them, as a favor, to do this price check.

I would appreciate your comments on this idea. Thank you.

MEMORANDUM HEADINGS

Like business letters, your memorandum stationery probably has not been re-designed for the past 25 years or more. And since this format is so frequently used for a wide range of interoffice communications, perhaps it is time for a cosmetic change that would have your employees take notice of your messages with a little more enthusiasm.

The following are typical memo letterheads. They are not exactly attention-grabbing, instead they are rather dull and commonplace.

MEMORANDUM

INTEROFFICE MEMORANDUM

OFFICE MEMORANDUM

Inter Office Communication

Dull

Vitality and originality are needed to improve the office memorandum's image. This can be accomplished by adopting a new typeface for your letter-head. There are several contemporary and attractive letterheads available from any shop where you have your memorandum printed.

In addition to a new letterhead, you might think about adopting a clever logo design for your memorandum to liven up your messages. Logo design

Inter Office Memorandum

Memorandum

Inter Office Memorandum

Memorandum

OFFICE MEMO

Inter Office Memorandum

Memorandum

Inter Office Memorandum

MEMORANDUM

Improved

can be found in a number of books that are available in most printer's offices. There are many universally-accepted logos, on a wide range of themes, that would be appropriate for any business communication.

The above are samples of letterhead designs. They are only a few of the more attractive designs that are available to suit your needs.

THE WEEKLY NEWS SUMMARY

One way that many companies have been able to cope with the growing numbers of memos that are written daily is to have a weekly news summary, bulletin, or newsletter that is used to convey information to employees in place of the numerous memos that go out on a daily basis. Using this format, many managers have told their employees that when they have a notice of general interest, it is to be sent to the person who is in charge of writing this weekly news bulletin or news summary, and it will be included in that rather than circulated in a separate memo. According to an informal survey of several businesspersons, the weekly newsletter has been an effective way to eliminate many of the daily memos.

The purpose of this weekly newsletter is to keep the employees informed as to policy matters, personnel changes, and practical information necessary to their job performance. It is often written by a person who has had little or no training as a writer. The publication is one that will be looked at quickly and discarded. It must contain easy-to-read, relevant information that is presented in an interesting and entertaining style.

The manager who finds himself/herself in the position of having to write a newsletter has a dual problem. He/she must attempt to develop two skills simultaneously: the ability to write with clarity and understandability, and the ability to keep an audience or readership interested in what he/she has to say. The key to success when confronted with the task of putting out a newsletter is to develop a "Nose for News."

Generally the stories in the newsletters will fall into these categories:

Special business news, trends, operations
Company policy
Appointments
Financial reports
News of special meetings (past or future)
Personnel information — anniversaries, leaves, etc.
Calendar of events
Special interest items e.g. bowling league results

When a department or company decides to utilize a newsletter format, it should seek input from all of its employees about the contents of the publication. In addition to providing a format for the airing of company policy matters, the newsletter should be a vehicle of information that is sought after by its readers. They should be offered the opportunity to suggest stories and even write some of the material when possible.

THE MASTHEAD

The newsletter's name is an important factor. It is the identifying symbol of the communication and, once selected, will remain with the newsletter forever. Choosing a name for a newsletter involves imagination and creativity without becoming carried away. For many situations the straight *XYZ Company's Weekly NEWS* is perhaps most appropriate although it may appear to be a bit dull. The following are some suggestions for newsletter titles. The list is by no means complete. It could go on for pages.

XYZ COMPANY'S WEEKLY NEWS
NEWSLETTER
NEWS BULLETIN
NEWS FLASH
NEWS AND VIEWS
XYZ NEWS IN REVIEW
MONDAY MORNING NEWS
COMPANY COMMENTARY
HIGHLIGHTS AND HAPPENINGS
COFFEE BREAK
etc.

It is important that the final masthead be designed by a professional graphic artist who will make sure the correct size, typeface, and design is chosen. This will be the identifying label of the newsletter forever. It should be chosen with care.

Garber Travel, a corporation of over 250 employees, started a publication called the "Monday Morning News" in the 1970s. According to the company's directors, the newsletter has been an invaluable aid in cutting down on the numerous memos that would be necessary to let the various travel agents know about trips and rates.

Monday Morning News covers all of this material and more. Sections such as the "Airline News," "Hotel News," operations, are invaluable aids to the travel agents who would otherwise need to be notified of these offerings and rates via the interoffice memo. The newsletter also includes personnel notices, bowling league results, and a pull-out section in a different color paper that is used by the accounting department.

One of the reasons for the high readership of the Monday Morning News (almost 100 percent of those receiving it responded in a survey that they read all or at least more than 50 percent of the publication) is probably the eye-catching covers that are designed by the company's graphics department each week. Note in the following examples the creativity and cleverness with which these covers are put together.

MONDAY MORNING NEWS

EDITOR: MARY DARLING

DATELINE: OCTOBER 20, 1980

LINDBLAD TRAVEL

Lindblad Travel offers a most unusual series of escorted tours to unusual and exotic destinations including:

CHINA - EGYPT
ANTARCTICA
AFRICA - SIKKIM
GALAPAGOS
(There are others.)

You have been visited (or soon will be) by Mr. Fernando Maldonado, our distinguished Area Sales Manager. Please listen to his descriptions of the Lindblad product.

He is available – and will appear with interesting films at local gatherings of people whom you think may be potential Garber/Lindblad clients. (See next page for list of travel films).

For further information about this and to break space – and for special attention to your clients, do not hesitate to contact Mr. Maldonado. Tel: (617)369-6688

Make sure, please, that your office is supplied with Lindblad's colorful brochures.

Recommend Lindblad to those of your clients who are looking for something unusual. <u>You</u> can recommend them with full confidence.

Foreign Sales in Brookline will be happy to help you with additional information.

One of the 12 huge marble statues of the Imperial Ministers dating from the 15th century. Along with lions, camels, horses, elephants, and mythical beasts, they line the avenue leading to the Ming Tombs.

MONDAY MORNING NEWS

EDITOR: Mary Darling

DATELINE: APRIL 14, 1980

TRIP OF THE WEEK

G W V   S P A I N   I B E R I A
WIDE BODIED JET RT
TRANSPORTATION

From New York and Boston
Starting April 14, 1980

ONE "GREAT" WEEK   TWO GREAT WEEKS
COSTA DEL SOL   THREE GREAT CITIES
(TORREMOLINOS)   MADRID-SEVILLE-TORREMOLINOS

$1 3 0   pp doub. occ. $2 8 5 pp doub.occ.

PLUS AIR   PLUS AIR

A copy of the GWV flyer is attached to the MMN. Flyers are in the mail from GWV.

We have included this program in our ad in Sunday's Boston Globe. The ad this week is large and features the same programs we advertised two weeks ago, with the exception of SPAIN, which is new. The MMN of March 31 describes these programs in detail.

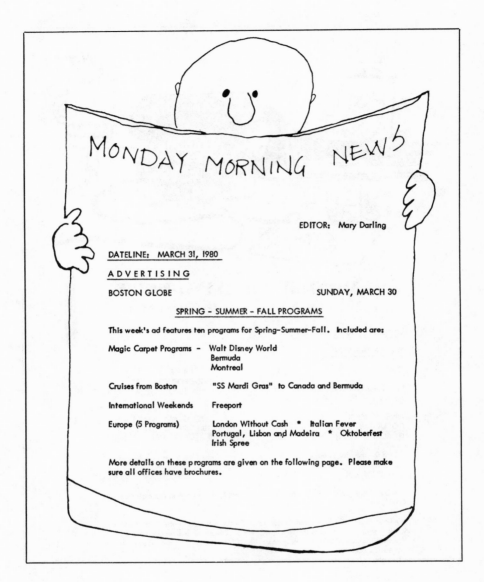

MONDAY MORNING NEWS

EDITOR: Mary Darling

DATELINE: MARCH 31, 1980

ADVERTISING

BOSTON GLOBE   SUNDAY, MARCH 30

SPRING – SUMMER – FALL PROGRAMS

This week's ad features ten programs for Spring–Summer–Fall. Included are:

Magic Carpet Programs –   Walt Disney World
                          Bermuda
                          Montreal

Cruises from Boston   "SS Mardi Gras" to Canada and Bermuda

International Weekends   Freeport

Europe (5 Programs)   London Without Cash   *   Italian Fever
                          Portugal, Lisbon and Madeira   *   Oktoberfest
                          Irish Spree

More details on these programs are given on the following page. Please make
sure all offices have brochures.

MONDAY MORNING NEWS

EDITOR: Mary Darling

DATELINE: MARCH 17, 1980

IRELAND 1980 THE IRISH SPREE

ONE WEEK	10 DAY	TWO WEEK
From $269 to $379	From $449 to $479	From $699 to $789
April 12 to Oct. 4	May 17 to Oct. 20	May 17 to Oct. 20

PLUS AIRFARE

SUPER APEX FARE $379 RT

Include hotels, daily breakfast, some meals, escorted daily luxury motorcoach sightseeing, hotel service charge, taxes and gratuities. Rates vary with date of departure. Frequent departures. Rates per person, double occupancy.

DUBLIN – OTHER CITIES – THE IRISH COUNTRYSIDE – Presented in BRIAN MOORE's inimitable manner.

Sunday's Boston Globe has the ad.   LET'S SELL THE IRISH SPREE !!

Happy St. Patrick's Day!

SPOT CHECK ON MEMO WRITING

1. Do I need to write this memo? Can the message be sent by telephone or in person to avoid the paperwork?
2. Have I carefully checked my list of readers to be sure my memo is only going to those persons to whom it is important?
3. Have I written my memo in the best possible style?
   a. one idea to a sentence
   b. no extra words and wordy phrases
   c. a clear, forceful creative approach
4. Would a picture say more than my words?
5. Is my style the best for this memo or can I condense my material by using numbered sequences, subheads, etc.?
6. Is it time for my company to change the letterhead of the memo stationery?
7. Would a weekly newsletter or bulletin better serve the company's needs and cut down on the number of memos we circulate?

9

The Search for Facts

Business cannot remain stagnant. It must constantly be on the look-out for new ideas, new data, new applications of old information. In some companies, whole departments devote endless hours to the search for new data and information necessary for planning future business activity. The pursuit influences major business decisions, employment practices, production methods, and even what is being produced.

For practical purposes, business research can be divided into two main types: pure research and applied research. Most businesses are concerned with applied research; that is, the programs that solve an immediate problem or answer a specific question, and that have a direct effect on the business.

Finding and analyzing facts and putting that data into a cogent, well organized written communication is a task assigned to many managers who are given little direction in the "fine art of communication." There are many tips on how to conduct that research that may be helpful.

ATTACKING A RESEARCH PROBLEM

Conducting research involves a plan of attack. The person assigned the task of writing a business report must know clearly what it is he/she is going to write about. The first step, therefore, is to define the problem. Write out the question to be researched or the conclusion to be reached so that the work has a direction and a specific focus.

Once the particular problem is outlined, the research plan calls for a list of the areas to be covered. Breaking down the subject into various areas for study shows the researcher what questions he/she needs to investigate.

The next step is to select the appropriate research methods. There are two classifications of source materials that a researcher will use in the study:

1. Primary sources. These are first-hand observations of a problem and may emanate from laboratory experimentation, direct interviews, surveys by means of a written questionnaire or an oral interrogation, or the personal examination of records and other available materials.
2. Secondary Sources. These are the written observations of others who have interpreted materials relevant to the subject being investigated that the researcher will read, synthesize, and borrow for inclusion in the report.

KEEPING A LOG

Many business reports are simply the translation of the "benchwork" of the laboratory scientist or engineer to a written document. The research method does not have to be analyzed in any great depth. It is actually the day-to-day findings of the employee that he/she must translate into a written format.

The simplest way in which a technical person can facilitate the reporting requirements is to keep an extensive log of the experimentation, which he/she is then able to transfer into the required report. If he/she is organized in his/her laboratory work, and he/she keeps accurate records, he/she will be able to communicate the progress to his/her superiors without too much difficulty.

THE INTERVIEW AND THE SURVEY

Other "first-hand" research techniques such as the interview and the survey require a different type of expertise. To conduct a successful interview the researcher must be adept at conducting a face-to-face meeting with another individual or a group of individuals. He/she must come away from that meeting with the answers to those questions which he/she needs to know. There are certain basic techniques to conducting a proper interview. They include:

1. Do your legwork in advance. Come into the interview with a basic knowledge of the subject at hand.
2. Prepare a list of questions to be asked at the interview.
3. Stay in control of the interview. Don't let the topic of discussion wander. Be sure you ask the appropriate questions and get what you came for by keeping the discussion centered on the topic you need to know.

A far more popular way by which business managers obtain first-hand information for a particular business report is to turn to the questionnaire or survey. A survey is only as good as the questions in it. There are some basic techniques to writing a good survey that a person must master if the research is to be worth anything.

1. Build in a variety of questions. There are various types of questions that a survey can employ and these should be included in the survey to provide a maximum output of information.
   a. The yes, no question.
      Example: Have you worked as an
               engineer before?
               _____ Yes? _____ No?
   b. Questions asking for a simple fact.
      Example: How many years of experience
               do you have _____?

c. Multiple-choice question.
   Example: Indicate the number of
            years of college training
            had.
            _____ None
            _____ 2-4
            _____ 5-8
   Example: How would you rate the
            company's in-house training
            programs:
            _____ Very Good
            _____ Good
            _____ Average
            _____ Poor
            _____ No Opinion

2. Be sure that the questions, when you mentally answer them, give you the input that you are seeking.
3. Be sure that the questionnaire is constructed in a way that will allow for fairly easy analysis of the results.
4. Make sure there are not too many open-ended questions requiring long answers.
5. Avoid confusing questions that the reader might have to stop to figure out.
6. Arrange the questions in a sensible order so that the reader follows your line of thought and does not get confused.

TIPS ON TAKING GOOD NOTES

In using secondary sources for research such as company records, books, periodicals, and other written materials, a researcher's most important tool is the ability to take good notes that will be useful in drafting the report.

Notes must be legible, logically organized, and easily understood. The most efficient way to take notes is to use index cards that can be numbered in the corner and shuffled around when it comes time to write. The names of the books and other references should appear on each card so that you can refer back to the source if necessary. There are several basic sources that a business researcher might want to be familiar with. The following pages contain some good examples of such sources.

REFERENCES/PERIODICALS

Periodical indexes of libraries contain alphabetized subject listings on any given business or industrial subject. The most helpful indexes are:

Business Periodical Index	Business, industrial, trade
Applied Science and Technology Index	Engineering, trade, business
Reader's Guide to Periodical Literature	General
Humanities Index	History, economics, political science
New York Times Index	*New York Times* newspaper including business section
Funk and Scott Index of Corporations and Industries	Corporate and financial reports on industries and businesses in U.S., Japan, Canada, United Kingdom
Applied Arts Index	Architecture, engineering
Poole's Index to Periodical Literature	Articles written 1803 – 1916

There are also several periodicals specifically for business including:

Business Week
Duns Review
Fortune
Harvard Business Review
Journal of Business
Nation's Business

Besides these major business periodicals, the library may contain copies of other magazines and journals pertaining to specialized areas of business in such fields as:

accounting
agriculture
advertising
data processing
economics
computer technology
industry
insurance
labor relations
legal matters
marketing

> office management
> personnel
> retailing
> the pure and applied sciences

The U.S. Government also publishes several indexes that could be helpful in doing research. "The United States Catalog of Government Publications" is issued monthly and, at the end of the year, an annual index is published. Also available are various pamphlets and bibliographical listings from the Government Printing Office.

BOOKS

The four chief sources for books include:

1. The library catalog
2. H.W. Wilson Company's *Cumulative Book Index*
3. *The United States Catalog* which lists all books published prior to 1928
4. *Publisher's Weekly* — a journal listing all books published each week

There are also available on the paperback bookshelves such helpful guides as *Basic Tools of Research* by Philip H. Vitale, which lists almost every guidebook, dictionary, bibliography handbook and index available.

Other reference materials which might be helpful include:

Corporate Directories such as:
Moody's Investment Service
Poor's Register of Directors and Executives
Standard and Poor's Corporation Services

There are also such directory references as:
Automotive and Aviation
Chemical and Engineering
Coal and Mining
Drugs
Electronics and Data Processing
Food and Food Processing

Encyclopedias particularly helpful to business include:

The Accountant's Encyclopedia   Financial information
The Columbia Encyclopedia   General, nontechnical

Encyclopedia of Banking and
Finance

Fortune Directory

Handbook of Advertising Management

These basic tools of research are available in all large, general libraries and may be found in the libraries of your own company. When writing a business report, even if it is a very specific report pertaining to a specific business problem, a little bit of research will go a long way. The additional information that you might pick up by reading an article in a periodical or finding a book on the subject might be just the right touch to put the report into the perspective that it needs. Sometimes a bit of history or a mention of a current issue or controversy will make the difference between dull reporting and a persuasive important communication.

SPOT CHECK ON RESEARCH

1. Do I have a "plan of attack" for researching my report?
2. Have I thought about the sources for my research? Will I use:
    a. Primary Sources e.g., first-hand observation.
    b. Secondary Sources e.g., books, periodicals, etc.
3. If my report is to be based on my own research, have I kept an appropriate log that could be written up into a formal report?
4. Have I considered the other options open to me in collecting research data:
    a. the interview
    b. the questionnaire
    Do I know how to use these tools effectively?
5. In conducting my research from secondary sources, have I taken adequate notes that I am able to logically transfer to written data?
6. Do I know how to gain maximum advantage from the research sources available to me?

10
Writing the Business Report

A report is a written communication that transmits information to persons interested in the information. Unlike business letters and memos, the business report concerns a subject that cannot be treated briefly or lightly. They are generally longer than a mere few pages and involve investigation, analysis, research and documentation.

TYPES OF BUSINESS REPORTS

There are several types of business reports that managers need to be aware of. They include·

> Policv Statements
> Periodic Reports
> Progress Reports
> Credit Reports
> Sales Reports
> Committee Minutes
> Public Relations Reports
> Annual Reports
> Attitude Surveys
> Advertising Reports
> Accounting Reports
> Market Surveys
> Personnel Reports
> Statistical Analyses
> Labwork Reports
> Product Analyses
> Readership Studies
> Research Reports

Reports can also be divided into two categories: *formal reports* and *informal reports.* The type of report is dependent upon several factors, including:

1. Complexity and treatment of the material
2. Length
3. Interest to the reader
4. Purpose and objective to be accomplished
5. Time for preparation
6. Permanent or temporary value of the report
7. Formality of the relationship between the reader and the writer
8. Intended use of the report

Informal reports generally are from three to ten pages in length and focus on subjects of current or temporary interest. They are intended for the purpose of keeping people informed or speeding up the progress of a particular action. They usually do not have any long-term impact and generally do not need a title page, table of contents, or summary section.

FORMAL REPORTS

Formal reports are obviously longer and more involved than informal reports. They contain many parts in addition to an introduction, body and conclusion; such as a summation, recommendations, and an appendix that might have several illustrations. Formal longer reports also must contain a list of the sources of information and should give an historical background of the subject being discussed. Often a longer formal report will contain acknowledgements and a glossary of terms. A detailed explanation of the parts of a longer report include:

Contents

1. Cover
2. Title Page
3. Notice — (indicates copyright of materials, permission to publish, etc.)
4. Forward — describes the report's purpose in being published and the completeness of subject coverage — the parameters of the report (or summary)
5. Abstract — summarizes the contents of the entire report. States the thesis, then the principal subtopics discussed in the report in the order of their discussion. (This is a key section of the report and it is particularly important that this section be written in the clearest possible language.)
6. Letter of Authorization — this is the warrant under which the report was written — can be in letter or memo format.
7. Letter of Transmittal — similar information to the forward but highlights key sections of the report and emphasizes key points the writer or research team feels are important.
8. Table of Contents
9. List of Illustrations
10. List of Tables
11. The Body of the Report

Text

The body of the report contains an introduction, followed by a section of conclusions and recommendations, followed by a body of back-up material.

The body of the report might consist of: (1) an expanded Three-Part Summary; (2) a process description section; and (3) the appropriate conclusions.

Each business organization has its own style and form for reports. Style and form may also vary somewhat within a company by department and by the nature of the subject being treated. Some may be so technical in nature that the body of the report contains many statistics, graphs and charts, and is almost organized in outline form. Others are mainly narrative with a minimum of tabular matter.

Before the report can be written, a good deal of preliminary work must be done. The investigator must define the purpose and determine the scope of the report. He/she must gather reliable facts and assemble and analyze them. He/she must draw conclusions from the factual analysis and make recommendations that are reasonable in view of company needs.

The purpose answers the question why was the report written. It must be clear in the writer's mind before he/she attempts to put his/her thoughts on paper.

The scope of the report sets its limits and narrows the subject to a logical and workable undertaking.

No report is stronger than the facts behind it. In gathering information and documenting it, a writer should be familiar with the authoritative references in this field. After the material relating to the topic has been collected and studied, the writer can begin to organize the report. Note cards should be reviewed, sorted by topic, and tentatively organized into a logical sequence for the report.

Using organized note cards as a guide, the writer should make an outline to serve as the structure or framework of the report.

Organizing

Before writing the outline, the writer of a report must arrange the material into some sort of logical pattern so that it will flow easily from one section to another. This process is called classification of data. There are four kinds of data:

Qualitative   — facts and ideas on a subject collected from research
Quantitative   — data expressed in numerical terms
Chronological — data arranged according to a time sequence
Geographical   — data classified according to regions of the world

The reasons to separate this data are fairly obvious. By doing this it will be easier to write the final report, inserting the necessary materials as needed. By weeding out the data that is quantitative, you can make judgments whether or not you might need charts and illustrations to explain your hypotheses. From the data you have gathered, you can determine the length and the focus of the report. By weeding out the chronological data, the writer can determine whether or not he/she wishes to arrange the facts in the order of their occurrence, and whether or not the time sequence should be given emphasis.

When the materials have been separated into categories it is time to begin the outline. A carefully prepared outline serves as a guide for the entire report. From it, the writing of the report draft should flow very easily.

Writing the Introduction

The good writer will write objectively, forming his/her statements from the facts found in the research. The introductory section of the report will tell the reader why it was written. The purpose of this section is to present the necessary background for the reader to understand the report. It may contain authorization or circumstances under which the report was requested, the need for this particular study and its intended use. It may delve into the history of the problem or may explain the purpose, objectives, scope and limitations. Sometimes the introduction also contains definitions of terms used in the report, and an explanation of the research methodology.

The Text

In the section labeled "Purpose and Scope" the writer of the report explains the basic objectives of the report. It is here that the writer presents the facts and gives the interpretation. Here, the report may be broken down into various factors to be considered. Here, the subject presented is discussed fully, presenting all aspects of the problem and the reasons for this discussion. It is also here that the writer must maintain complete objectivity, "reporting" only that which is fact. Any bias will weaken the impact of the report. Although it is true that all reports can be slanted by means of what is included or omitted, it is in the purpose and scope of the report that the writer must remain objective and eliminate all value judgments.

The Ending

In the conclusions and recommendations section of the report, the writer should refer back to the purpose of the document. For each purpose stated, there should be a conclusion or a recommendation. Obviously, it is here that the writer's value judgments are woven into the presentation. Although a necessary part of the recommendations, they should be based on the facts presented and not merely the opinions of the writer. Good, valid conclusions, are inferences that the writer makes from the information presented. Their strength depends on the validity of the information and the logic on which they are drawn. In other words, value judgments are only valid if they are supported by concrete evidence. A weakness of many reports is the "hasty generalization," a sweeping statement not supported by evidence. Writers are advised to check their reports for these easily developed flaws and to make sure that each conclusion or recommendation makes logical sense.

The recommendations of the report pertain to the action that is to be taken as a result of the report. They are supported by the conclusions and attempt to answer the points stated in the purpose of the report. They may be treated in a numbered list or in paragraphs, and should answer the questions:

> What is to be done?
> Who is to do it?
> When it is to be done?
> Where the action is to take place?

Usually, recommendations are the last section in the long formal report, although they may be placed at the beginning. It is up to the writer to determine where the recommendations will be the most effective. Remember, many business reports are written for a busy reader or skimmer who goes over the conclusions and recommendations quickly and hurries on to another matter, leaving the details to a subordinate to check. If the conclusions are at the beginning, there is a greater chance that they will come to the attention of the person you desire to reach. This decision is also based upon the type of report you are distributing. Most reports are either "investigative" or "advisory." Information reports summarize facts, and their conclusions are pretty obvious. Those reports that are advisory, on the other hand, have a stronger purpose that needs immediate attention. They tend to be less objective and impersonal.

STYLE

The report should be written in a style that allows for a logical order and sequence. The ideas should be set forth in some sort of sensible arrangement so that they follow one another. The actual writing style of the report should be as close as possible to the principles of clarity, conciseness and coherence. Particularly in a technical report, the writer must be concerned with explaining his/her point so clearly that any potential reader will understand the explanations. The key to this is to use straightforward simplicity — short sentences, short paragraphs. The writing style may actually be choppy and contain repetition. It will certainly lack any of the polish and finish of fine prose. But it will convey its point so that it is unmistakably clear. A checklist for writing contains the following:

1. Are my ideas clear, so clear that there is no mistaking what I am trying to say?

2. Do I have all my ideas in the proper order for presentation?

3. Do I need a case study for illustration?

4. Do I need tables or graphic illustrations?

5. Does the text of my report flow easily from one idea to another?

6. Have I buried any of my essential details or facts in the mass of text?

7. Does the report contain a sense of completeness, a feeling that it has covered the subject thoroughly and there is no need for further investigation?

8. Is the report an appropriate length in view of the subject matter?

9. Can the reader skim this report and get a sense of what I am trying to say?

THE APPEARANCE OF THE REPORT

Unlike the other business writing formats, the report requires not only advance preparation and good writing but neat assembly as well. Since the business report consists of a number of different elements, they must be put together in such a way that the document is a complete unit that is attractive and easy to follow. The details of format such as spacing, numbering, captions, and style and arrangement on the page will differ from one independent writer or one company to another. However, there are some essential parts of the report that must be included if it is to succeed in its communication function. In order of appearance, the parts of the report fall into this sequence:

1. Preliminaries
2. Text
3. Reference Materials

The preliminaries include the cover, title page, letter of transmittal or foreword, and the table of contents. The cover attracts the attention of the reader and protects the documents. It should be durable enough to withstand wear and tear and simple enough so that it does not appear to be ostentatious. The title page should include the title of the report, the name of the author, and usually the name of the company and the date the report was issued.

A long report is usually accompanied by a letter of transmittal or a foreword. This section explains the reasons why the report was written and who authorized it. It might refer to some of the sources of research and acknowledge those individuals or institutions that were helpful in compiling the report.

In a report of more than a few pages, a table of contents is essential. This provides the reader with a succinct way of determining what sections he/she needs to pay special attention to and gives him an "at-a-glance" overview of what he/she is about to read.

The text of the report contains the body of data, the issues discussed, the conclusions and recommendations. The reference materials, which can be several pages, include appendixes containing illustrations, graphs, charts, explanations, a bibliography, and even an index in a very long report.

Reports are usually typed on white bond paper, either single- or double-spaced. Double-spaced reports are easier to read and more pleasing to the eye than those that are single-spaced, and all reports should have ample side and bottom margins. With the exception of page numbers, no words should invade the margins.

A long report benefits from having a number of headings and sub-titles, especially in the text. These heads should be typed in all capital letters and are often underlined as well.

Pages should be numbered beginning with the title page. In the preliminary section of the report the pages are numbered with consecutive Roman Numerals. In the text they are numbered in consecutive Arabic Numerals beginning with 1.

A general rule of thumb in designing a report is to use plenty of white space. Do not try to economize at the expense of a cramped appearance. The report is not in a contest for an advertising prize so do not try to lure your reader with a lot of fancy gimmicks. The message should be presented in a neat, organized fashion, with an understated rather than overstated design. Organization is the key, and a listing of elements is one way to achieve clarity.

SPOT CHECK ON BUSINESS
REPORT WRITING

1. Have I met the three criteria for report writing:
    a. Is my report a useful instrument?
    b. Does this report serve to improve my organization in any way?
    c. Does this report indicate the scope and ability of the person doing the reporting?
2. Is my report properly organized?
3. Is my title effective? Will it lure the reader into the report?
4. Can my reader understand the essence of my report from the summary section of my introduction?
5. Is the report complete or have I left anything out?
6. Is my research capable, and does that factor come through in the report?
7. Do I need visuals to give further explanation or emphasis to any of my major points?
8. Does the report leave me with a sense of completeness? In other words, have I tied up all the loose ends?

11
Communicating Visually

"Sometimes a picture is worth a million words."

Seeing things visually is one of the first cognitive experiences of most human beings. It is the way we remember our childhood. It is the way we learned the letters of the alphabet and the numbers that were the basis of our education.

Visual communication is the sending of messages by using picture images. These may be in the form of charts, graphs, symbols and photographs that are flashed before our eyes. In the 1980s, visual communication will realize its full potential with the increasing influence of television, and the use of computer graphics to convey messages that used to be in oral or printed formats. Because we are surrounded by these visual influences and have learned to think visually, we need to rethink even the presentation of written reports.

Visual aids in written communication convey meaning and specific explanation essential to effective business communication. They help us to understand and remember more easily. They improve the appearance of written messages, and support the important points made in the document.

CHOOSING VISUAL AIDS

There are several factors on which to base the selection of the visual aids that are to be included in business reports. They include:

1. the type of report
2. the purpose of the report
3. the data to be presented
4. the reader's background and knowledge
5. the amount of data (particularly quantitative data) to be discussed

In certain reports, the use of visual aids is essential in presenting a clear and understandable message. In the annual report, for example, charts and tables are able to translate the complex dollar figures that must be sent to the stockholders. Reports that deal with involved sales figures, or advertising and promotional materials, also use graphics for clarity.

When using visuals, consideration must be given to the reader of the report and his/her ability to comprehend particular charts and tables. The chart must be organized in such a way that the reader can grasp the material quickly and easily. The purpose of the visual is to save the reader's time. If it is not understood "at-a-glance," it is useless.

Types of Visual Aids

There are many tables, graphs, charts, and other graphic forms from which to choose in preparing visual aids that will go into your report. Usually these aids are prepared before the final report is assembled. You must then decide whether the visuals should be incorporated into the report as a whole or included as an appendix.

Tables

A table is a graphic way of presenting information systematically arranged in columns and rows. It simplifies the display of a large number of items, helping to summarize numerical and statistical data, or to show comparisons, trends, and quantitative data in an easily readable fashion. There are three types of tables: general reference, special purpose, and text.

EXAMPLE OF A GENERAL REFERENCE TABLE

Employee Holdings in Company

Name	Salary	Stock Holdings (%)	Benefits
John Doe	$125,000	.35	29.0
Jim Taylor	118,000	.55	32.0
Caren Connor	114,000	.62	39.0
Robert Jones	110,000	1.24	62.0
Ginny Murphy	92,000	3.57	31.0
Carolyn Thimes	87,000	.73	19.0
Thomas Carrie	72,000	.19	2.0
David Maxwell	69,000	2.42	41.0
Carroll Conlon	62,000	.27	3.7
Reid Rodney III	60,000	3.15	18.0

EXAMPLE OF A SPECIAL PURPOSE TABLE USED IN A REPORT

SURVEY OF EMPLOYEES
"Monday Morning News"

Question	Percentages		
	Always	Sometimes	Never
1. Do you receive your "Monday Morning News" each week?	100.0	—	—
2. Do you read the complete Newsletter each week?	85.0	13.0	2.0
3. How often do you refer to the travel information?	73.0	22.0	5.0
4. Do you find the personnel notes to be significant?	66.0	32.0	5.0
5. Is the format easy to follow?	93.0	6.0	1.0

EXAMPLE OF TEXT OR SPOT TABLE

	Yes	No
In favor of more input	68%	32%
Interested in reading matter	42%	33%
Want more classes	83%	17%
or		
25% responded favorably		
62% responded with a maybe		
13% made no comment		

The general-reference table presents detailed information for reference purposes. For example, the tabulated results of a questionnaire might be shown in a table placed in the appendix of a report or a proposal.

The special-purpose table covers only specific points about a particular issue or problem. It is not as inclusive as a general reference table.

The text or spot table displays a short single group of facts or figures and is handled like a paragraph insert.

Charts

A chart is the presentation of data in a graphic form other than tabular. The data are plotted on a graph, or mapped to show relationships. Charts reinforce a message by simplifying the important points. They leave a visual image with the reader. Charts use lines, bars, curves, columns, blocks, and pictoral symbols to illustrate their point. The best charts tell a story with no explanatory notes in the text of the report. Although they may have accompanying explanation, they can stand alone.

Probably the most common charts are bar charts. They are used widely in advertising and promotional material, and are effective for comparing different items of a specified date. Bar charts can either be horizontal or vertical.

There are also line and curve charts. These are often called graphs. They are charts in which items of data are plotted out in connecting points by a line or a curve. They are useful for depicting something that takes place over a time period, and often can be used to display more than one item, by using several lines plotted along the same framework.

In company annual reports and other official documents "Organization and Flow Charts" appear with frequency. They show the flow of authority, responsibility, and information among the positions in a particular firm.

There are also pie charts that present data in the form of a circle. The circle is divided into the pieces of a pie, and each of the pie's segments represents a particular bit of information.

SIMPLE BAR CHART

Earnings Per Share

1980	5.32
1979	5.00
1978	4.73
1977	3.42
1976	2.10
1975	1.98

EXAMPLE OF A LINE CHART: CORPORATE GROWTH

Customers in hundred thousands ▬▬▬
Income ▬ ▬ ▬ ▬

EXAMPLE OF AN ORGANIZATION AND FLOW CHART:

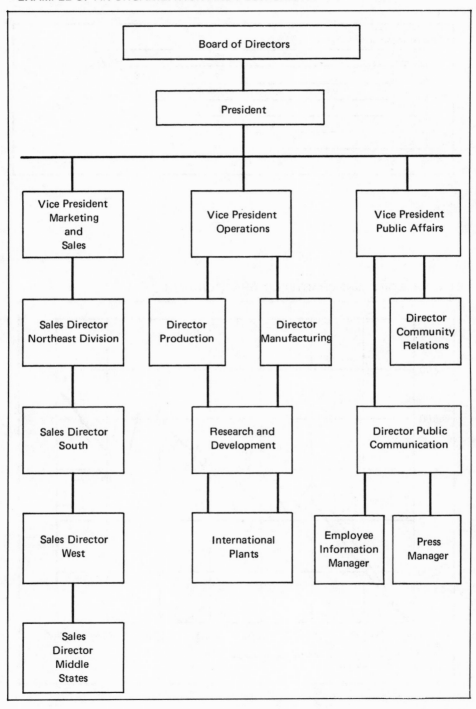

EXAMPLE OF A PIE CHART: UNIONIZED EMPLOYEES

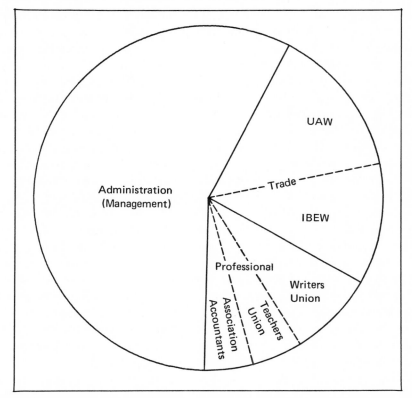

Several other graphic illustrations that may accompany reports and proposals include maps, diagrams, and photographs. These visuals lend interest to the report, and break up the long paragraphs of copy with a pictoral message that is an important part of the final text.

GETTING THE MOST FROM YOUR VISUALS

Generally, visuals used in the body of the report help to explain the text. When they are placed in the appendix they are used for reference purposes. In most business communications it is preferable to use visuals in the body of the text. This will help to hold the reader's interest and break up the lengthy text. When this tactic is used, however, the visual should be as closely related to the text as possible, and large tables that occupy whole pages should be avoided. When using several tables or charts, they should be numbered consecutively throughout the report. There should always be a caption or explanation phrase underneath the table.

Remember, visuals are not ends in themselves, but are merely means to explaining and clarifying the data in a report.

USING VISUALS IN ORAL PRESENTATIONS

The purpose of using visual aids in oral presentations is similar to the purpose of using them in written communications; that is, to increase the understanding of facts or data being discussed. In other words, these aids serve to clarify, to interest the listener, or to support what is being said.

The most common methods of presenting visuals in an oral presentation include the use of chalkboards, flip sheets, and felt boards. They are the least expensive and require no prior knowledge on the part of the speaker to be operated effectively. In all of these supplementary pieces of equipment, the presentation of the visual depends upon the ability of the communicator to clearly present the visual so that it is not a hastily scribbled mess. The graphs, charts, and tables drawn out on these surfaces need to be carefully planned in advance so that they help to coordinate the entire presentation. They need to be placed so that they are visible to the entire audience, and ultimately serve as an asset to the speech, and not a liability.

Other common visual aids used in presentations include overhead projectors or opaque projectors. The transparencies for this equipment have to be prepared in advance of the speech, and the speaker has to be familiar with the workings of the projectors. Adding materials to a particular visual while the audience watches is an effective way to hold the audience's attention. Overlays can be added to the transparencies, with favorable impact. Any materials such as graphs, charts, tables, and photographs can be placed on transparencies for projection. They are easily and inexpensively designed.

More complex visual aids used in speeches include slide/tape presentations, television and motion pictures, and an ever-increasing number of graphic applications using a microcomputer. These visuals, however, are costly and complicated to use, often creating difficulty for a speaker who is not adept in using the equipment.

Visuals are supposed to enhance, not detract from communications. Used properly, they are extremely effective in adding interest, vitality, and excitement to a message. Used ineffectively, they can cloud the issue and botch the most polished of speeches. However, it is important for the business communicator today to include visuals when preparing a long document for consideration.

SPOT CHECK ON VISUALS

1. Have I considered the use of visuals in my document?
2. Will a table help me to explain some complex data that would be confusing in narrative form?
3. Would a chart enhance my presentation?
4. Do the visuals I have planned belong in the body of my copy or in an appendix?
5. Have I properly numbered-coded my visuals so that they will fall into proper place?
6. Do I understand how to use visuals effectively in oral presentations.
   a. chalkboards, felt boards, flipcharts . . .
   b. an overhead projector and transparencies
   c. slide/tape equipment
   d. motion picture films
   e. television videotapes

12
Writing the Business Proposal

The business proposal is a format designed to request funding from a particular source or group. Its purpose is to present, in clear, lucid, and persuasive terms, why your idea warrants the expenditure of a significant sum of money to implement the plan that you are proposing.

This chapter shall deal with the document loosely referred to as a "proposal" by managers. This is distinct from the funded proposal, in which a company or institution applies to a funding source such as the government or a foundation for financial support for a project. The funded proposal must meet rigid requirements not expected of other written formats. The "business proposal" we are talking about is a more informally structured document, often in the form of a budget presentation, or a reorganization plan. However, many of the same characteristics are found in both the funded proposal and the business proposal, so that the subsequent suggestions can be utilized for both.

Virtually all proposals have one objective — to sell someone on some idea that needs financial support. As a result, all proposal documents must be persuasive. They must make a compelling case for the idea or action to be undertaken. Since good projects do not, of themselves, guarantee funding, the writer of the proposal must make the clearest, most coherent case if he/she is to get what he/she wants.

ELEMENTS OF THE PROPOSAL

Generally, a proposal consists of several essential parts. They include:

> Title Page
> Abstract
> Problem, Statement or Statement of Need
> Objectives
> Procedures
> Facilities, Equipment, Personnel Section
> Budget

The Title

The title of the proposal should clearly state the premise. The title page should include the title of the project, the name of the person making the proposal, the organization and dates of the project, and the total budget request.

Choose a title for your proposal that reflects the objectives of the project, and gives the reader an idea of what the project is all about. Keep it as short as possible while attempting to inject some imagination and flair into it. Don't be "cute" in setting up your title page but don't be dull either. Select a design that is lively and interesting. Keep away from the simple white page with black print.

The Abstract

The abstract is a crisp summary of the overall project. It must include all of the major points of the study or project, and should outline the objectives, procedures, and evaluation process in brief terms. The abstract should be between 200 and 500 words, and every one of those words counts. This is the section in which you sell yourself and your ideas. You must present the purpose, scope, and significance of your proposal in such a way that the reader will want to continue reading. You must answer the questions, "Who," "What," "Where," "When," "Why," "How," so that key officials in the company will immediately grasp the importance of your project without reading through the entire proposal document. The stress in the abstract is on the ultimate objective or end product of your work. All of your best writing skills and editing skills must be put to the test in composing the abstract.

The Problem Statement

This section includes a clear, precise statement of the problem to be addressed. It talks about what needs to be done and why it needs to be done. It relates the problem to a particular need for answers.

It is in the problem statement that the writer must illustrate that he/she has a complete understanding of the project he/she is proposing, and its relationship to the company or the organization he/she is working for. It is here that he/she must show the importance and significance of the project, its timeliness, and its ultimate worthiness to the company. It is here that the writer must indicate his/her own understanding of this project and his/her particular ability to handle it. If this is a budget request, asking for monies to support new services or research, the writer must explain and support each item under consideration. If the proposal is to purchase a new data processing system, the writer must demonstrate why a new system would be preferable over already existing capability. If the proposal is to suggest a reorganization of a division or department, once again, the writer must show the interrelationships between the present situation and the improved future situation as a result of the proposed reorganization. It is here that you indicate whether or not you have done your homework, whether or not you have thoroughly researched your problem before submitting the proposal. If the statement of need is weak, the project will be refused. If it is convincing because it is based upon thorough analysis and competent reporting of that data, then it has a fighting chance for a favorable outcome.

Objectives

The intended outcome of the project is covered in the "Objectives." This section is devoted to a long and detailed explanation of why you are suggesting this proposal, and what you see as the final outcome. This section should cover both general goals of the proposal, and specific concrete objectives. Often these goals and objectives can be stated in the form of questions that you will raise, and the answers that you intend to seek. Some of these questions might include the following checklist:

Will the project accomplish something significant?
Will the proposed outcome help to solve current problems?
Are the procedures being used adequate to carry out the intended outcomes?
Is the staff that has been suggested appropriate to the purpose of the project?
Are there enough objectives — not too few, not too many?
Can I accomplish what I have stated I will accomplish?
Is the outcome statement as short as possible?
Does the outcome fit the scope of the problem statement?

If the proposal writer is not clear on the objectives, then they will not be clear to the reader either. In writing the objectives, it is important to set the goals firmly in mind, and write them out in some sort of outline form so that they make sense. Leave no question in the mind of your reader as to what is the exact purpose of this request requiring company funds.

Procedures

This section of the proposal describes the methodology by which you will conduct your research. How you will accomplish your objectives and test your ideas are the questions to be answered in the procedures section of the proposal.

In writing the procedures, make sure that they coordinate with the outcomes that were suggested. Although some proposals may include objectives for which there are no procedures, it is important that there is a parallel between the outcomes and the procedures suggested.

It is also important in writing about the procedures to emphasize that there is a clear, logical rationale for each procedure that is suggested. The writer must convince his/her readership that he/she is not undertaking many unnecessary steps in solving the problems he/she must address in order to accomplish the proposal's stated objectives.

Facilities, Equipment, Personnel

The purpose of this section is to outline the space required, the equipment needed, and the necessary personnel to conduct the research for the proposal.

Be thorough. This is your one chance. You cannot come back to request additional space or people for the job after the proposal has been accepted. Be sure to justify all of the items that you list. Don't just gloss over your requirements for facilities, equipment, and personnel. Like the other components of the proposal documents, this section must show your organizational ability; a complete understanding of your idea and a total grasp of the requirements to do the job. Don't pad the proposal too heavily or it will overwhelm. Don't be too frugal in describing your needs either, or you will find yourself in a bind when you are faced with the completion of your task.

Preparing the Proposal Budget

Using graphs, charts, tables, and narratives, you must present a complete breakdown of the cost of the project, in the section entitled "budget." It is advisable to divide the budget considerations into specific categories, e.g. supplies, materials, equipment, personnel, data processing, etc.

Much time, effort, and painstaking detail must go into the preparation of the budget. It is here that you explain, in fiscal terms, the entire spectrum of your proposal. The budget will clarify confusion that might have stemmed from the listing of needs, or the details of the procedures and objectives.

Actually, the budget should be prepared during the process of organizing the proposal. As each item in the proposal is researched and suggested, a budget figure should be allotted to it. Once the written draft of the proposal is completed, the budget items should easily follow from these projections. Occasionally it is necessary to redesign a procedure or an objective to conform to a reasonable budget. Do this before submitting the proposal document. Don't leave unanswered questions, or room for argument or challenge, by submitting an inadequate budget. Don't plan to submit a partial budget, with the idea that you can always ask for additional funds in the future. Only a fool would believe that he/she could get away with that approach.

The budget should also reflect a complete understanding of company policy, and how money is expended for such items as telephone services, utilities, etc. Is there a central ordering department, or can materials be ordered for this particular project?

A typical budget sheet would look something like this:

Item	Total	Justification	Page Reference
Salaries	$100,000	Two technicians added to staff for lab work plus clerical assistance and project director.	Page 22, 23, 24

Item	Total	Justification	Page Reference
Supplies (lab)	1,800	Chemicals, test small #2 data machine, rotary circulator, etc.	Page 16 – 18
Supplies (misc.)	600	Mailing costs, stamps, office supplies including xerox etc.	Page 19
Telephone	1,200	$10 each month for 12 months	Page 25
Travel	1,600	Visits to other sites and attendance at meetings	Page 20
Research costs	5,000	Publications and other printed materials. Cost of a paid consultant during initiation of project.	Page 24
Miscellaneous expenses	2,000	Unanticipated inflation and increases in travel, supplies, etc.	Page 18

In summary, keep the following in mind when developing your budget:

1. Plan the budget along with the entire proposal. Develop the financial side of the picture each step of the way.
2. Make sure you thoroughly understand your project and reflect this in your budget.
3. Be sure you are aware of company policy and other regulations that might affect your project and your financial plan.
4. Be sure you can account for each necessary expenditure. Each budget item should be well documented, and the total budget should not project a figure that is unreasonable, or unrealistic.

WRITING STYLE

The writer of a proposal is trying to persuade another person or group that he/she has a worthwhile project that will enhance business and help the company. Essentially he/she is unfolding a narrative, and must construct a written document that has merit, interest, and intrigue. The experienced writer will begin the proposal with an introduction that will "set the stage" for what is to come. In his abstract, he/she will entice the reader into wanting to know more about the project, and its application to business improvement. The writing style, therefore, plays an important psychological role in determining whether or not this project will receive favorable action. Subsequently, it must be interesting, informative, and concise. In other words, like every other written business communication, the proposal, too, must be kept short. It must state, at the beginning, what the project is about, and what is to be accomplished, using the minimum number of words. Professional jargon and verbosity should be eliminated. Avoid sweeping generalizations, and grandiose promises that cannot be kept.

The proposal must be written in the objective voice, with the clear and logical analysis of facts needed to convince your reader that you have ability to carry out this project. The expertise of the writer should be obvious.

All individuals to be involved in the project should be discussed in the proposal. A brief explanation of their positions, backgrounds, and the role they will fulfill, should be included, in a convincing way, to show that they are qualified to work on this endeavor.

Also, the logic of the arguments you use in your presentation must be clear. This is one writing format where a certain amount of repetition, for emphasis, might be useful.

Another useful device in the written presentation of your proposal is to use as many graphs, charts, and tables as you can to reinforce your narrative, and help to synthesize it for your reader. These graphic devices are essential to an effective presentation.

It is also a good idea to use frequent sub-headings, underline key phrases, and space the text of the proposal, so that it is open and easy to read. This will ensure that the person who only intends to give the proposal a "quick review" will be attracted to the key points in the presentation.

Obviously, a proposal document must not have any spelling or typographical errors. It must be neat and clean, and grammatically correct. If the writer turns in a sloppy proposal, the impression he/she will leave is that he/she is liable to turn in sloppy work.

One of the most important concerns in putting together the proposal is to ensure that there is a logical flow of ideas from one section of the proposal to another. The document must make sense. It must hold together as a unit so that there is no confusion as to the ultimate goals. Repetition of certain items and good use of transitional devices and sub-headings will help to keep the presentation well organized and flowing properly.

SPOT CHECK ON PROPOSAL WRITING

1. Am I able to answer the question: Who is my proposal document aimed at and have I met the criteria to sell this individual (or group) on my ideas?
2. Is my title page effective?
3. Have I given the proper time and editing skills to my abstract so that anyone reading it will immediately understand the key points of my proposal?
4. Is my problem statement comprehensive enough to give my reader a complete picture of my proposal?
5. Does it indicate my expertise and ability to handle the problem?
6. Are the objectives clear?
7. Do the procedures I discuss make sense when viewed in light of my objectives?
8. Have I been thorough in my description of facilities, equipment, personnel, or do I need to go back and recheck this section of my proposal?
9. Is my budget reasonable, complete, sensible? Is it adequate to do the job, but not so generous as to be wasteful?
10. Have I used a writing style that is pompous and verbose, or have I managed to communicate my proposal in clear, persuasive terms?

13
Oral Presentations

With palms sweating, knees knocking and butterflies growing larger and larger in your stomach, you're about to make a speech. Except for the format and style, there is really no difference between preparing an oral presentation and preparing a written message. You still have to be in command of the basics; you have to know precisely what you're trying to accomplish; you have to master the subject; you have to organize your thoughts; you have to structure the flow of your ideas, for maximum effectiveness.

THE AUDIENCE

In spite of the butterflies, sweating palms and knocking knees, fear not. Any audience can be won over with a little work. They are, after all, just individuals like yourself and not a group of calculating persons who are sitting in judgment of your every word and movement. So before you write, keep these fundamentals in mind. Ask yourself: What do I want the listener to know, or believe, or do? Am I simply giving this presentation to inform the company's Board of Directors about a new project we have undertaken? Am I here to persuade this Board that they should adopt a new policy? Is this a presentation designed to merely educate or teach, or do I expect some action to result from what I am trying to say?

The manner and methods utilized in the oral presentation depend upon the ultimate goals of the speech. If you are looking for a reaction from your listener, then the atmosphere must be electric with discussion and response. If you are just fulfilling a required obligation to inform, then your presentation need not be as dynamic and suspenseful. The point is that you tailor the language and the props used in the presentation to the particular end you have in mind.

In analyzing your audience, consider their background and understanding of what you are talking about. Think through how much jargon common to your business they will understand. Do you have to define the technical terms you're planning to use, or are you both "tuned in" to the same channels as fellow members of the same company, institution or profession? Consider, too, whether or not this is an audience that requires a "hard sell" approach. If you are directing your talk to your own Board of Directors, you tread a fine line between a "hard sell," "soft sell," and the appropriate balance to convince them of your ideas, and your importance to the company.

USING VISUALS

Finally, when considering the audience, think through how you can use visuals to effectively enhance this particular speech, for this particular group. Before you write a word for the presentation, determine when and where visuals might fit in.

In selecting these visuals, your choices are limited by the physical location of the presentation. However, in most rooms you can use a flip chart, felt sheets, or an overhead projector. There are usually plugs for slide equipment or other audio/visual machinery. Don't complicate your presentation by using visuals that will create a problem for you in terms of mechanical difficulties, but don't overlook the impact of visuals either. They often add a great deal to what would be a boring, dull presentation. They provide an outlet for explaining complex charts, graphs, and statistical materials that would be confusing if presented any other way. So consider putting your graphs or charts on transparencies, and using an overhead projector to help you explain a particularly complex section of your presentation. If an overhead projector is not possible, use a flip chart to try to accomplish the same purpose.

Often you will prepare advance copies of sections of your presentation that you will hand out to the audience, once again to help you explain a particularly complicated set of statistics. These hand-outs can be used in addition to visuals, or in place of them

WRITING THE ORAL PRESENTATION

Like most other forms of writing, the speech has an introduction, a body, and a conclusion. The introduction is crucial. Here is where you establish contact with the audience. Here is where you either arouse interest and develop a receptive audience, or you promise boredom and create an apathetic, sleepy, perhaps hostile audience. Remember that the reader of a written communication can stop reading at any time if the introduction doesn't grab his/her attention. The listener of a speech, on the other hand, is trapped into remaining in the room. He/she can only be angered by the "waste" of time he/she is required to "suffer." So you must arouse interest, establish a rapport, get your audience to accept your message. Be sure to draw attention to your subject, and not to you, personally, the speaker. Make sure that your opening is relevant to your subject.

Some devices for effective openings:

1. Refer to an event that is of major importance to the audience, or of major interest. For example, when doing a presentation for the company's Board of Directors, refer to a current economic concern that would be important to the company's business. Start the presentation with a quotation from a recent article from a magazine or journal, and launch your discussion from that point.
2. Start the presentation with an illustration, a story, or an anecdote. Make sure, however, that you do not get involved with a story or anecdote that is trite or foolish. It must have some significance to your overall purpose

3. Ask an important question, or make a startling statement to launch your presentation. Wake up the group right from the start by making them sit up in their seats and start thinking about what you have to say.

There are other common ways to open your speech. For example, you can refer to the occasion for the meeting; you can begin with a personal greeting; you can simply state the subject of the presentation and plunge right in. These openers will not arouse immediate interest and are not the preferred way to begin. They will, however, get you off the hook when you are groping for an opener.

One type of introduction to *always* avoid is the apology. Such a negative opening prepares the audience for a second-class performance. If you remind the audience that you are "stage-struck" or that your speech was hurriedly prepared, they will notice that and stop listening to the rest.

Never begin the speech with such an unsubtle remark as "I thought I would talk about . . ." Seem childish to you? It is, and must be avoided.

The length of the introduction will vary in proportion to the body of your speech. Your opening remarks should set the tone and the pace for the presentation. Don't lose the audience here, or you may never recapture them.

The body of the speech, obviously the longest, is similar to the central portion of any written piece. Once you have introduced the theme and captured the attention of the audience, you have to accomplish what you set out to do; that is, to inform, persuade, educate, prompt to action, etc. Here is where you lay out your facts. Here is where you present all of your arguments, statistics, definitions, analyses.

All the public speaking techniques in the world will not help you with your oral presentation if you do not have something that is worth saying. In the body of the speech, get right into this central portion of your presentation without a lot of fanfare and frivolity.

It should be obvious by now that an effective oral presentation must be written out before it can be presented orally. Organizing the body of the presentation is much like organizing the body of a report. All of the facts must be put together in a coherent fashion so that they make sense; so that one idea follows another, and serves as an introduction to the idea that is coming. The body of a speech needs the proper transitional links between thoughts, just as the body of a report needs the proper transition between paragraphs.

The best way to organize the body of the speech is to prepare an extensive outline, which helps you to meld the proper ideas together, and to look at a total picture to see if you have included everything you need. From this outline, you might want to transfer your thoughts to 3 X 5 or 5 X 8 index cards, which you will actually use in the presentation. Generally, it is not necessary to write out the entire speech, although for some people this is the only way they will feel confident about the ultimate presentation. Whether or not you write out the body of the speech, never memorize it. Your presentation will be too stiff and formal if you read or recite from memory, and it will lose some of its impact. The best speech is the one that is well thought out, and well rehearsed. The speech writer must have complete command of the subject, and be able to communicate that knowledge to the audience, using all of the visuals and devices that have been prepared.

If, in the body of the speech, you must deal with technical words that need explanation; or with statistics that need a graph or chart for clarification, prepare a hand-out that you can ask your audience to refer to as you talk. This will prevent you from stumbling unnecessarily over material that is hard to explain. It will assist you in retaining the interest and understanding of your audience.

The ending of your speech is probably the most crucial portion of the presentation. It is true that the opening establishes the contact between the speaker and the audience and paves the way for a receptive, interested group of listeners, but it is in the ending that you will make the lasting impression that will test the true effectiveness of what you had to say.

If action is called for, your words must be stirring. If protest is called for, your last words must be demanding of thought. If you are pleading a case for a budget authorization, your last words must be strong, forceful, convincing. In other words, your conclusion must stir your audience to have the precise action that you are seeking. It must capture the very substance of your theme, and must wrap up all the unanswered questions.

Your conclusion is your last opportunity to persuade the audience that you have something worthwhile to convey. Don't lose that opportunity with an offhand remark or a trite expression.

When you determine what your conclusion might be, write it out and memorize it so that you will not forget those important words. This is, however, the *only* section of the speech that you should memorize.

THE MECHANICS OF THE PRESENTATION

There is no magic to being a speech maker. Like any other form of communication, the magic is in the hard work that goes into the preparation. The first element in this preparation is to know the subject. A good speaker must have such a complete grasp of the topic of the presentation that no question will stump him/her; no snag in the presentation will upset him/her; no controversy will stop him/her from making his/her point.

A speech must be heard, not read. Therefore, it does not have the advantage of being reread so that the audience can fully digest the main points.

There are no subheads in a speech, no titles, no paragraphs, no punctuation marks and italics.

On the other hand, a speech does have the advantage of the speaker himself — his appearance, his personality, his voice, his eyes. When delivering a speech, there should be one-to-one contact between the speaker and the audience so that the speaker can see and feel if he or she is losing or boring the audience. He or she can also tell if the audience is responding to the discussion. He/she can raise his/her voice, gesture, whisper, or repeat a point if necessary.

Since the speech involves the speaker as a human being, it is well to note that the speaker's dress is important. His or her appearance should fit in with the accepted mode of dress for the particular organization. Clothing that is too loose, too tight, too loud, or too sedate is inappropriate on the day you need to deliver an oral presentation. It is also wise to avoid shoes that are uncomfortable and jewelry that jangles or distracts. Most speakers have difficulty deciding what to do with their hands. If you are not using visual props, which would occupy your hands, keep them evenly placed on a table or podium, using only a minimum of hand gestures.

One of the most important qualities in giving an oral presentation is enthusiasm for your subject. If you are not completely convinced of the sincerity and importance of your topic you will have difficulty convincing others. With the proper voice inflections, and a genuine inner feeling of conviction for your topic, you will succeed in conveying your message to others. One good way to practice your speech is to tape your presentation and listen to how it sounds. You will immediately pick up those qualities that are good and bad from a tape that hides nothing. Another effective way to conquer your fear of presenting this speech and overcome your wonder at how you look is to practice in front of a mirror — it, too, tells no lies!

FIELDING THE QUESTIONS

Often at the end of a speech the audience will be asked to direct questions at the speaker. Most good speakers invite questions from the audience. They are so confident of their ability to handle the topic of discussion that they welcome the opportunity to clear up any problems.

Try to answer all questions directly, honestly, and simply Be brief, but be explicit. If you run into a hostile questioner, do your best to consider his/her points, and reply with courtesy. Under no circumstances do you resort to combating hostility with your own hostility. This would not serve any purpose but to antagonize an audience, which up to this point, might have been with you all the way. If you are faced with a question that you cannot possibly answer, don't try to fake an answer. It is always better to admit that there is something you do not know than to bluff your way. The audience will spot a bluff fairly rapidly. When asked a question that you cannot answer, offer to jot down the name of the questioner and find the answer for him/her.

SPOT CHECK ON ORAL PRESENTATIONS

1. Have I analyzed my audience so that I understand how to construct my oral presentation for this particular group?
2. Have I taken into account the need to explain all jargon and technical terminology?
3. Have I done a good job of determining where and when visuals will be useful to me in this presentation?
4. Do I need to prepare my hand-outs?
5. Is my introduction captivating and inspiring, or do I need a good "gimmick" to launch my presentation?
6. Have I prepared an extensive outline of my presentation and properly organized this talk?
7. Do I know my subject completely so that no new angle can be thrown at me that I cannot anticipate and respond to?
8. Is my ending effective so that I leave my audience with a lasting impression?
9. Have I rehearsed my speech with a tape and a mirror so that I am aware of how I will carry out the delivery?
10. Have I considered all of the necessary elements to making a favorable impression, including the details of dress and appearance?
11. Am I prepared to face the questions I will be required to respond to at the end of the presentation?
12. Do I have a generally good and confident feeling about my speech, which I will be able to convey to others?

14

Communicating by Computer - The Challenge for Tomorrow

Banking by telephone, shopping by computer, instant retrieval of information from a central storage facility, these were pipe dreams fifteen to twenty years ago.

Now automatic teller machines allow customers to conduct banking transactions, including deposits, withdrawals, borrowing and repaying — without talking to a human being.

Customers can call computers to learn how to repair their own appliances; newspapers are experimenting with "electronic delivery" of the news directly into a home television screen; various institutions are building a central data base of information that can be retrieved by computer terminal, including direct access to information on subjects from the latest stock and bond quotations, to the names and menus of local restaurants.

In medicine, doctors are experimenting with the computer to spot neurological disorders like multiple sclerosis. They are using computers to analyze blood samples, and even to put together some basic facts to come up with a diagnosis for such things as infertility.

Over a century ago an English mathematician, Charles Babbage, designed a machine that was based on certain principles of electronics. His idea was to develop a really powerful tool that would handle any mathematical computation automatically. Little did Mr. Babbage know, in 1882, that his machine was the forerunner of a bunch of wires and circuits that would revolutionize society.

The "age of the computer" really began in 1939 when Dr. Howard Aiken of Harvard University completed plans for a calculating machine that utilized many of the principles used in today's computers. The first, big electronic computer was built in 1946. It was called ENIAC (Electronic Numerical Integrator and Calculator); it filled a huge room, utilized 140,000 watts of electricity, and contained 18,000 vacuum tubes that generated and controlled the electrical current that enabled ENIAC to calculate.

The discovery of the transistor in 1947, and then the subsequent discovery of the semiconductor chip in 1959, or "miracle chips" as they have been called, once again advanced the industry. These little specks contain a calculating capability equal to the ENIAC. With this miniaturization of parts, amazing feats have become possible.

The result is an "information industry" that is growing at a rate of 20 percent annually — an industry that is expected to grow into a $500 billion-a-year enterprise during the decade of the 1980s.

What this means is "change!" Change in the way business will do its "business." Change in the way business will communicate to its customers, its employees, and to the public at large.

The word processor is quickly replacing today's standard typewriter. A word processor is a machine that provides the office with a very fast means of document production, revision, and typing. It has the capability for fast information retrieval from its memory unit, and can be linked directly to printers, processors, photocomposition systems, computer input microfilm systems, optical character recognition scanners, and computerized dictation systems. Using telephone lines, several word processors can be linked together to communicate with one another.

The era of the word processor marks an end not only to the standard typewriter, but to the mountains of papers and carbon copies that have to be stored in file cabinets, which take up so much space. Digital storage of the small word processing discs requires less space. Automated information retrieval is far quicker.

It has been estimated that one-third of total office costs are in the preparation, duplication, handling, and storage of paper. U.S. industry has over 26.5 billion documents in storage. This glut of paper has been spawned only since the mid-1950s. While the cost of maintaining this paperwork has doubled over the past decade, word processing costs have steadily decreased. This inevitable change appears to be preferable both from a practical and economic viewpoint.

Electronic mail brings another change to the business office of tomorrow. Still in its infancy, electronic mail ultimately will create a totally new way of communicating those letters, memos, and short reports that are a daily task for many managers.

Today, most business messages begin as long-hand drafts or dictation, followed by typing, revision, and retyping. Most of this work, except for the initial dictation, is done by a secretary, and copies are made on a copier machine for dissemination and eventual storage. With electronic mail, the originator, i.e. the manager, will be transmitting the message at a video display unit directly, without the services of a secretary. The advantage of electronic mail is in its directness and speed. Changes and revisions are made right on the video screen as you compose. Electronic mail is expected to "humanize" the process of business communications. But it means that the manager will need to be more aware than ever before of correct English usage, good grammar, correct spelling, and a good writing style (although already, the computer has the ability to correct grammatical errors and spelling). As is true of word processors, storage of electronic mail messages is on small discs, and is easily retrieved since the computer, not a clerk, looks for the information.

Another standard of today's office — the telephone — will also be different in the office of the future. Telephones are being replaced with two-way video display terminals that not only have speech capability, but also facsimile and graphic display. The telephone network, with its various copper, microwave satellite, and optical links, is and will continue to be the major communications network for office communications. In addition to providing a vehicle for computer-to-computer talk, facsimile and communicating word processors, it will have the capacity to perform many other important functions. One of these is to provide on-line visual access to information stored anywhere in a company's computing telecommunications network, so that any location — home, automobile, poolside — can become an office. Some have projected that the business executive will carry his/her office with him/her in an electronic briefcase, consisting of a screen, a touch-sensitive keyboard painted on plastic, a control unit, and one or more chip storage units, holding whatever information is needed.

The systems available today are only the crude forerunners of what is to come. The computer is already a fixture in the office of the 1980s. Its influence reaches out to every segment of society — education, transportation, business, and commerce. More than one million computer systems were in operation as of 1980 — seven times as many as were in operation in the mid-1970s.

Since the computer is able to build information on layers of previous information, and these bits are stored in memory units, the computer can provide answers to all kinds of questions, with incredible speed and precision. To be sure, computers will not provide answers to all of the complex problems of the business world and society at large. And they will bring problems directly attributable to their presence.

These "smart machines" will cause widespread dislocation for many workers who will be displaced when full automation takes place. Traditional businesses, such as television networks and publishing companies, will encounter great competition as automation is beamed directly into the home and the office. There will have to be a massive retraining of personnel, so that secretaries can become the word processing technicians of tomorrow, and clerks can be redirected to other functions. Even the role of executives will change as they are forced to think at a keyboard, and conduct meetings over a video terminal.

Will computerized communications result in better communications? Better management? Better interpersonal relations? This is an unknown. It represents an awesome challenge for every manager, to see to it that a better way lies ahead.

Appendix:
A Handbook of Helpful Tips

RULES OF ENGLISH GRAMMAR

In English, there are eight traditional parts of speech. Each word is classified by the way in which it is used in the sentence.

The Parts of Speech

1. Nouns
A noun is a word that names a person, place, thing, action, quality, or idea.
  a. Nouns are of two types:
    (1) Proper nouns that so precisely identify an object or idea, that it is set apart from all other similar objects or ideas.

      James Smith
      New York City
      America

    (2) Common nouns that identify a general class of objects or ideas.

      man
      table
      love

  b. Words used as nouns serve as subjects or objects in a sentence. They also serve as appositives (words that emphasize or explain other words by repeating — just as this parenthetical expression is doing) to other nouns and to pronouns.

2. Pronouns
A pronoun is a word that stands for a person, thing, or idea, without specifically naming it. A pronoun replaces a noun and performs the same function. The eight types of pronouns are as follows:

Personal:	I, you, he, it, my, yours, his, its, me, him
Relative:	Who, which, that, whoever, whatever
Demonstrative	This, that, these, those
Indefinite	Each, either, any, some
Interrogative:	Who, whom, whose, which, what
Reflexive:	Myself, yourself, himself
Intensive:	Myself, yourself, ourselves
Reciprocal:	Each other, one another

3. Verbs
A verb is a word which describes action, state of being, or feeling. Verbs tell what a subject does, is, or feels, and may indicate how an object is affected by the subject. Verbs have five important qualities.
  a. Tense. The time-showing quality (past, past perfect, present, present perfect, future, or future perfect).

Past:	I *took* the test.
Past Perfect:	He *had taken* the course of instruction.
Present:	He *takes* good care of his camera.
Present Perfect:	You *have taken* a good approach to the problem.
Future:	You *will take* CPR training beginning next Monday.
Future Perfect:	By this time tomorrow I *shall have taken* my final examination.

b. Voice. The quality which shows whether the subject acts or is acted upon.

| Active: | He *hit* me. |
| Passive: | I *was hit*. |

c. Mood. The quality which shows whether the writer regards the statement as a fact, as a wish or possibility, or as a command.

Indicative:	He *will be* here today.
Subjunctive:	If he *were* here today, we would go.
Imperative:	He *shall be* here today.

d. Person. The quality which shows whether the speaker, the person spoken to, or the person spoken about, is affected (first, second, or third person).

	Singular	*Plural*
First person:	I go	We go
Second person:	You go	You go
Third person:	He goes	They go

e. Number. The quality which shows whether the verb refers to one or to more than one person, thing, or idea (singular or plural number — see example above).

4. Adjectives

An adjective is a word which describes or limits a noun or pronoun.

A *hot* day	*This* object
A *tall* drink	*His* dog
A *smooth* stone	*Several* women
A man	The *English* ships

5. Adverbs

An adverb is a word which describes or limits a verb, an adjective, or another adverb.

a. Adverbs are commonly used to tell how, when, where, why, how much, and to what extent.

Highly praised organization
Widely practiced policy
Steadily held
Quite readily identified

b. Adverbs are often adjectives or participles to which the ending ly has been added. However, many adjectives are also used as adverbs without a change in form. For example, *fast, better, much,* and *straight.*

6. Prepositions

Words which relate a noun, a pronoun, a phrase, or a clause to another element — or a sentence are prepositions. The noun which follows a preposition is its object.

A verb:	We *placed* him *in* the *cage.*
Another noun:	Hear the *noise of* little *voices.*
An adjective:	We are *rich in knowledge.*

7. Conjunctions

Words which join words, phrases, or clauses are conjunctions.

a. Coordinating conjunctions connect two or more sentence parts of equal rank. For example:

Both children, *Karen and Keith,* wanted to go, *but neither the teacher nor the principal* would *approve and give* permission for the idea.

b. Conjunctions that introduce dependent clauses and join them to main clauses are subordinating conjunctions:

We felt *that they would join us if they could, because* they were also interested in the proposal.

8. Exclamations

Any word used independently to show strong feeling is an exclamation.

What!　I can't believe it.
Stop!　The area is restricted!

The Parts of the Sentence

A sentence is a group of words which expresses a complete idea.

The subject of a sentence names the person or thing which does the act or about which the statement is made.

The bottom line comes first.
Product X was a good item.
We should have taken the left turn.

1. Complements

Often the subject and verb are so complete in themselves that they require nothing else to constitute a sentence (I will go). Frequently, however, some other sentence part is needed. A complement is the noun or adjective (or their equivalents) which rounds out the meaning of the verb. There are four kinds of complements which occur regularly in the common sentence patterns of English.

The direct object follows only verbs of action and designates the person or thing that directly receives the action. It answers the question *whom?* or *what?* after the verb.

>He prepared the *report.*
>He hit the *bull's-eye.*

The indirect object names the person or thing from whom or to whom the action is performed. It answers the question *for whom?* or *to whom?* after the verb. (A verb which takes an indirect object also will always have a direct object.)

>He sent *us* our *orders.*
>I gave *him* my *proposal.*

The subjective complement is a noun, a pronoun, or an adjective that renames or describes the subject. Subjective complements follow verbs of being and other linking verbs.

Noun:	Our greatest concern is *security.*
Pronoun:	It is *she.*
Adjective:	The company was *tired.*

The objective complement is a noun, a pronoun, or an adjective that refers to or describes the direct object. In a sentence with an objective complement, the infinitive *to be* is present or may be inserted between the direct object and the objective complement.

>Most Americans think our government to be the world's *best.*
>The committee made him their *spokesman.*

2. Phrases

Sentences may also contain phrases and clauses, which are groups of words that function as single units.

   a. A prepositional phrase is composed of a preposition and its object.

   (1) Ordinarily, the object is a noun or pronoun, or sometimes a group of words used as a noun or pronoun.

>He shouted from the *ridge.*
>We told him to give it *to whomever he wished.*

   (2) A prepositional phrase may be used as a noun, adjective, or an adverb.

Noun:	The worst time is *after sundown.*
Adjective:	We could see the edge *of the lake.*
Adverb:	We left *in a hurried fashion.*

b. Verbal phrases are phrases composed of verb forms (verbals) with their modifiers and complements. Verbals, with their complements and modifiers, are used as other parts of speech — nouns, adjectives, or adverbs. There are three kinds of verbal phrases: participial, gerundive, and infinitive.

1. A participial phrase is composed of the present or past participle of a verb and its complements or modifiers. A participial phrase always functions as an adjective.

Selling at the convention, the company received good reviews on its new product.

2. A gerundive phrase is composed of a gerund and its complements and modifiers. A gerundive phrase always functions as a noun, an adjective, or an adverb.

Teaching business communications is not always easy.

3. An infinitive phrase is composed of an infinitive (plus the verb root) and any modifiers and complements. It may be used as a noun, an adjective, or an adverb.

Noun:	*To be a good instructor* requires hard work.
Adjective:	We now have the capability *to capture the East market.*
Adverb:	He arose *to explain his idea* to the Board.

3. Clauses

A clause differs from a phrase in that the clause has a subject and a predicate. There are two types of clauses: independent and dependent (subordinate). An independent clause may stand by itself as a sentence. However, a dependent clause, like a phrase, does the work of a single word; it may serve as a noun, an adjective, or an adverb.

a. Noun clauses have the following uses in a sentence:

Subject:	*Whatever he does* will always be done right.
Subjective complement.	That is *what he told us.*
Delayed subject:	*It* has been determined *that we cannot move.* (*It* is an expletive.)
Direct object:	We think *that you are mistaken.*

Object of Preposition:	He can send it by *whoever is going.*
Preposition:	His feeling *that the fight would go in our favor* was justified.

b. Adjective clauses may modify nouns or pronouns.

We took the position *which led to bankruptcy.*
Was it they *who asked you?*

c. Adverbial clauses show their adverbial function by telling one of the following things about the predication: how, when, where, why, how much, or to what extent.

You may start *after we give the signal.*
He set up his stand *wherever he could find an audience.*
We were so tired *that we couldn't walk another step.*
If they attack, counterattack.

Types of Sentences

Sentences may be classified, according to their makeup, into the following four groups:

1. A *simple* sentence consists of one independent clause; it may, however, have a compound subject or a compound verb, or both.
2. A *complex* sentence consists of one independent clause and at least one dependent clause.
3. A *compound* sentence consists of two or more independent clauses.
4. A *compound-complex* sentence consists of at least two independent clauses and at least one dependent clause.

PUNCTUATION

The Period

1. Use a period, with two typing spaces following, to end a declarative sentence.

The company lost $10 billion in sales last year.

2. Use a period to end an imperative sentence.

Lock up when you are finished.

3. Use a period at the end of a polite request phrased like a question.

Will you please look over this report and meet with me tomorrow on it.

4. Use a period after the initials of a name.

M.H. Carrino

5. Use a period after most abbreviations.

   (e.g.) Mass. St. Corp.

6. Use three spaced periods (. . .) or ellipsis points to show that you are omitting words from a quotation.

   "To know is nothing at all . . " (Anatole France)

7. Use a period for the decimal point in figures.

   $5.95   6.5 percent

8. Use a period after the identifying elements of an outline.

   I.
     A.
     B. etc.

9. *Do not* use a period:

   After roman numerals in a sentence.
   After a letter used to identify an object or indicate a fictitious person.
   After *percent*.
   After chemical symbols.

The Question Mark

1. Use a question mark with two typing spaces following at the end of a direct question.

   How can profits be improved?

2. Use a question mark at the end of a sentence that asks a question, even if the form is declarative.

   The risks are too great?

3. On sentences that are part question, part statement, use the end punctuation suggested by the final clause.

   The union does not wish to listen to reason but even if they considered it, would it make any difference?

   What should we do, although I do not want to think about it.

4. A question mark is sometimes used to indicate doubt about the accuracy of a statement.

   They have been a client of ours for 35 (?) years.

The Exclamation Point

1. Use at the end of a sentence to express strong feelings.

   The company is out of business, as of now!

   Use sparingly, overuse diminishes effectiveness.

Quotation Marks

1. Use in typed copy which in printed format would be words in italics.
2. Use to indicate a slang word.
3. Use single quotation marks to indicate a quote within a quote.
4. Use to indicate what was said.
5. Punctuation with quotation marks. Periods and commas always are inside quotation marks, exclamations, dashes, etc

Question Marks

Question marks are placed according to the meaning conveyed.

The Comma

1. Items in a series — words, phrases, clauses, figures, signs — should be separated by commas. Use a comma before the conjunction that connects the last item in the series.
2. Use a comma between adjectives of equal rank. Don't use a comma if they are not of equal rank.
3. Use a comma before the conjunction in a compound sentence, except when the sentence is very short.
4. Use a comma to show the omission of a verb in the second part of a compound sentence.
5. Use a comma after an introductory clause or phrase.
6. Use a comma for clarity when there is a long introductory clause or phrase.
7. Use a comma after such expressions as "for example," "that is," "i.e."
8. Use a comma to set off the name of a person addressed.
9. Use a comma between the days of the week and the months, between the name of the city and state, between a name and titles that follow the name.
10. Use a comma after the complimentary close of a letter.
11. Use a comma after a question followed by a question.
12. Use a comma where needed to clarify elements in a sentence, but omit where there is no significant pause in the sentence.

Semicolon

Basically the semicolon functions as a weak period or as a strong comma. In general, avoid its use when a period would lend clarity; use in place of a comma, however, when a comma would not be enough of a separation.

The Colon

1. The colon is a mark to suggest something follows: what follows may be an explanation, a list or an example.
2. In a letter, use a colon after the salutation and to separate the initials of the person dictating and the person typing.
3. Use a colon also in stating the time, in citing a biblical reference, and to separate place of publication and publisher in a bibliography.

The Apostrophe

The apostrophe is used to show possession. In changing singular to possessive add the apostrophe and the letter. In changing plurals to possessive, use the letter and the apostrophe following. Apostrophes are also used to show contractions, e.g. can't, don't.

The Hyphen

The hyphen is used generally to show that a word is divided at the end of a line. Hyphens are also used between certain words that become apparent with usage or can be checked in a current dictionary.

The Dash

A dash indicates a sudden shift or break in thought. It should be used sparingly.

Parentheses

Usually, information that is not mandatory to the sentence but is explanatory in nature is enclosed in parentheses. They are also used when repeating a number for accuracy.

Italics

Titles of books, magazines, newspapers, plays, motion pictures, and long poems should be set in italic type or underscored in typescript or handwriting. Also set in italics are legal cases, the names of ships and aircraft, foreign words, cliches or slang expressions.

When to Capitalize

1. The first word of every sentence.
2. All proper nouns.
3. Names of religious, fraternal, and political organizations.
4. Titles used with a name or in place of a name.
5. The names of the days of the week, months of the year, holidays, but not the names of the seasons of the year.
6. The first and last words, and all important words in between, of titles of books, stories, poems, paintings etc.
7. The pronoun "I."
8. The points of the compass when they refer to sections of the country, but not when they indicate directions.

SPELLING HANDBOOK

Some Rules

If a one-syllable word ends in consonant-vowel-consonant, double the final consonant before adding a suffix that begins with a vowel.

Note these examples:

	Suffix	*New Word*
wrap	er	wrapper
ton	age	tonnage
hum	ing	humming
star	ed	starred
drug	ist	druggist
big	est	biggest
tag	ed	tagged
bet	or	bettor
brag	ing	bragging

This rule does not apply if the final consonant is not pronounced.

If a two-syllable word ends in consonant-vowel-consonant and is accented on the second syllable, double the final consonant before adding a suffix that begins with a vowel.

Here are some examples:

	Suffix	*New Word*
occur	ence	occurrence
refer	ed	referred
expel	ing	expelling
transmit	er	transmitter

defer	ed	deferred
begin	er	beginner
acquit	al	acquittal
repel	ing	repelling
admit	ance	admittance
allot	ed	allotted

Drop a final *e* before adding a suffix that begins with a vowel.

The rule implies that the final *e* should be retained if a suffix beginning with a consonant is added. Note the following examples:

	Suffix	New Word
hope	ing	hoping
excuse	able	excusable
please	ant	pleasant
scarce	ity	scarcity
desire	ous	desirous
choose	ing	choosing
like	able	likable
obese	ity	obesity
freeze	ing	freezing
excite	able	excitable

Because each suffix in the following list begins with a consonant, the final *e* in the root word is retained.

move	ment	movement
tire	less	tireless
remote	ness	remoteness
strange	ly	strangely
appease	ment	appeasement

After a soft *c,* write the *e* before the *i* when these two letters appear in sequence.

deceive   receive   conceive   perceive   receipt   deceit

Also write the *e* before the *i* when these letters are to be pronounced with the sound of long *a.*

sleigh   skein   heinous   inveigh   neighbor   vein   reign

In most words the *i* is written first.

believe   grieve   tier   mischievous   spiel   relief   shriek

Several common words represent exceptions to the general rule. The correct spelling of these words will demand individual attention:

forfeit   height   counterfeit   sleight   seize   weird

The following list of reference words are frequently misspelled. The list is intended for reference purposes only. It would be impossible for a poor speller to memorize them all. If spelling is one of your nemeses, learn to use a dictionary.

Troublesome Words

absence
absorption
accede
accessible
accommodate
accumulate
achieve
acoustics
acquittal
advantageous
affiliated
aggressive
alignment
allegiance
all right
aluminum
analyze
apparent
appraisal
appropriate
argument
assistant
auditor
bankruptcy
believable
benefited
campaign
canceled
canvass
category
changeable
clientele
collateral
committee
comparative
competitor
concede

connotation
consensus
convenient
convertible
copious
corroborate
criticism
crystallize
defiant
definitely
despair
development
dilemma
disappear
disappoint
disbursement
discrepancy
discriminate
dissatisfied
distributor
eligible
embarrassing
endorsement
envelop (verb)
eradicate
exaggerate
existence
extraordinary
flexible
fluctuation
gratuity
grievous
haphazard
hypocrisy
illegible
incidentally
indelible

independent
indispensable
insistent
intermediary
irresistible
irritable
judgment
judicial
labeling
legitimate
leisure
license
likable
litigation
maintenance
mathematics
mediocre
minimum
negligence
negotiable
noticeable
occurrence
omission
opponent
oscillate
outrageous
panicky
parallel
paralyze
permanent
perseverance
persistent
personnel
persuade
plagiarism
possesses
precede

predictable
preferred
privilege
procedure
pronunciation
psychology
pursue
questionnaire
receive
recommend
repetition
rescind
rhythmical
ridiculous
sacrilegious
salable
secretary
seize
separate
sergeant
stationary
stationery
strategy
succeed
superintendent
supersede
tangible
technique
tyrannize
unanimous
until
vacuum
weird
withholding

Geographical Locations

Mediterranean	Gibralter	Ukraine
Pennsylvania	Caribbean	Thailand
Saskatchewan	Pittsburgh	Pompeii
Albuquerque	Manhattan	Portugal
Schenectady	Bethlehem	Labrador
Massachusetts	Wisconsin	Ethiopia
Presbyterian	Honolulu	Antwerp
Rio de Janeiro	Aleutians	Columbia
Appalachian	Nicaragua	Morocco
Corpus Christi	Winnipeg	
Philadelphia	Milwaukee	Missouri
Los Angeles	Sioux City	Tennessee
Philippines	Louisiana	San Diego
Sacramento	Des Moines	Worcester
Nova Scotia	Minnesota	Abyssinia
Afghanistan	Savannah	Caucasus
Scandinavia	Allegheny	Marseille
Dardanelles	Melbourne	Shanghai
Chatianooga	Indonesia	Venezuela
Wilkes-Barre	Edinburgh	Adriatic
Chesapeake	Chile	Baptist
Jerusalem	Omaha	Filipino
Yugoslavia	Tucson	Niagara
Versailles	Hawaii	Delaware
Shreveport	Ottawa	Colorado
Terre Haute	Egypt	Oklahoma
Minneapolis	Sicily	Toronto
Connecticut	Tacoma	Paterson
Cincinnati	Quebec	Montreal
Baltimore	Vienna	Syracuse
Manila	Phoenix	Ontario
Roanoke	Potomac	Babylon
Aegean	Sahara	Panama
Yangtze		

ABBREVIATIONS

States and Territories

	Zip	Common
Alabama	AL	Ala.
Alaska	AK	Alas.
Arizona	AZ	Ariz.
Arkansas	AR	Ark.
California	CA	Calif.
Canal Zone	CZ	C.Z.
Colorado	CO	Colo.
Connecticut	CT	Conn.
Delaware	DE	Del.
District of Columbia	DC	D.C.
Florida	FL	Fla.
Georgia	GA	Ga.
Hawaii	HI	
Idaho	ID	
Illinois	IL	Ill.
Indiana	IN	Ind.
Iowa	IA	
Kansas	KS	Kans.
Kentucky	KY	Ky.
Louisiana	LA	La.
Maine	ME	
Maryland	MD	Md.
Massachusetts	MA	Mass.
Michigan	MI	Mich.
Minnesota	MN	Minn.
Mississippi	MS	Miss.
Missouri	MO	Mo.
Montana	MT	Mont.
Nebraska	NB	Nebr.
Nevada	NV	Nev.
New Hampshire	NH	N.H.
New Jersey	NJ	N.J.
New Mexico	NM	N. Mex.
New York	NY	N.Y.
North Carolina	NC	N.C.
North Dakota	ND	N. Dak.
Ohio	OH	

ABBREVIATIONS (Continued)

States and Territories

	Zip	Common
Oklahoma	OK	Okla.
Oregon	OR	Oreg.
Pennsylvania	PA	Pa., Penna.
Puerto Rico	PR	P.R.
Rhode Island	RI	R.I.
South Carolina	SC	S.C.
South Dakota	SD	S. Dak.
Tennessee	TN	Tenn.
Texas	TX	Tex.
Utah	UT	
Vermont	VT	Vt.
Virgin Islands	VI	V.I.
Virginia	VA	Va.
Washington	WA	Wash.
West Virginia	WV	W. Va.
Wisconsin	WI	Wis.
Wyoming	WY	Wyo.

Business Terms

a/c, acct.	account
a.m., A.M.	before noon
amt.	amount
assn., assoc.	association
asst.	assistant
bal.	balance
c/o	care of
Co.	company
c.o.d.	collect on delivery
Corp.	corporation
dis., disc.	discount
doz.	dozen
ea.	each
enc.	enclosure
etc.	and so forth
f.o.b.	free on board
frt.	freight
ft.	foot, feet

Inc.	incorporated
Ltd.	limited
mdse.	merchandise
memo	memorandum
Messrs.	Misters
mo.	month
mfg.	manufacturing
mgr., man.	manager
No.	number
pd.	paid
P.O.	post office
p.m., P.M.	after noon
P.P.	parcel post
R.R.	rural route, Railroad
sec., secy.	secretary
treas.	treasurer
wk.	week
wt.	weight
yd.	yard
yr.	year

TITLES AND SALUTATIONS

The President	Dear Mr./Ms. President
Assistants to the President	Honorable
The Vice President	Dear Mr./Ms. Vice President
The Cabinet	Dear Mr./Ms. Secretary
Legislators	Honorable
The Judicial Chief Justice	Dear Mr./Ms. Chief Justice
State and Local Officials Including Governors, Mayors, State Representatives and Senators	Honorable
President of Board of Commissioners	Honorable
Religious Leaders:	
Protestant Minister	The Reverend
Rabbi	Rabbi
Catholic Cardinal	His Eminence Cardinal
Catholic Archbishop	The Most Reverend
Catholic Bishop	The Most Reverend
Catholic Monsignor	The Right Reverend

TITLES AND SALUTATIONS (Continued)

Catholic Priest	The Reverend
Mormon Bishop	Mr.
Protestant Episcopal Bishop	The Right Reverend
Protestant Episcopal Dean	The Very Reverend
Methodist Bishop	The Reverend
Chaplain	Chaplain

Academic Officials:	
President of College (with doctorate)	Dear Dr.
President of College (without doctorate)	Dear Mr./Ms.
Dean of a school	Dear Dean

CLICHES COMMON IN BUSINESS

according to our records
acknowledge receipt of
allow me to state
and oblige
as per your request
assuring you of our prompt
   attention
at all times
at hand
attached please find
at this time
awaiting your favor
awaiting your further orders
beg to state
by return mail
contents duly noted
dictated but not read
enclosed herewith
enclosed please find

esteemed favor
even date
favor (as a synonym for letter)
for your information
has come to hand
in due course
keep our options open
recent data
same (as pronoun to stand for
   noun in previous sentence)
thanking you in advance
the undersigned
this letter is for the purpose
under separate cover
we wish to advise
we would ask that
would state
you claim, you say, you state

WORDY EXPRESSIONS

Instead of	Try to use
abovementioned	this, these
after very careful consideration	after considering
ahead of schedule	early

WORDY EXPRESSIONS (Continued)

Instead of	Try to use
along the lines of	like
apropos of the above	regarding, concerning
at such time	when
attached you will find	attached is
at your earliest convenience	soon, immediately, as quickly as possible
comes into conflict	conflicts
despite the fact that	even though, although
due in large measure to	due largely
due to the fact that	because
each of these	each
enclosed herewith is	enclosed is
for the purpose of	for
for the reason that	since
give consideration to	consider
give instruction to	encourage
give rise to	cause
have need for	need
if doubt is entertained	if doubtful
in a most careful manner	carefully
in accordance with	by
in a satisfactory manner	satisfactorily
inasmuch as	as
in the amount of	for
in the event that	if
in the case of	if
in the near future	soon
in view of the foregoing	therefore, hence, as, because
is of the opinion	believes
in large measure	largely
make inquiry regarding	inquire
make an adjustment in	adjust
of the order of magnitude	about
on the basis of	by, from
on the occasion of	on
of a confidential nature	confidential
owing to the fact that	because
prior to	before
subsequent to	after
take into consideration	consider

NUMERALS

Many numbers are used in business writing, and there are some general rules of style that lend clarity and commonality to their use. The following suggestions might help.

1. Most writers agree that the number "ten" and all numbers below should be written out because they are simple and easy to remember, and most other numbers should be expressed in numerals.
2. If a sentence begins with a number, the number should be expressed in words.
3. When two numbers are used to form an approximation, the numbers should be expressed in words.
4. When using a series of numbers, use numerals.
5. A dollar amount should be generally expressed only in figures.
6. When using long lists of complex numbers it is best to put them in some sort of tabular format so they are clearly expressed.

TIPS ON WRITING A GOOD RESUME

The major element in writing a good resume is organization. The ability to put together a set of facts in an orderly attractive fashion is all that is needed. All resumes cover basically the same general categories and should be set up as follows:

1. At the top center appears the name, address and telephone number of the person.
2. At the top right is the date.
3. Professional Objectives — This is probably the most difficult section to write. It requires the composing of one sentence that is clear, succinct and direct which states what it is you are seeking. This statement should be general enough so that you are not locked into a narrowly defined position but specific enough to represent your goals.
4. Education
5. Professional Experience
6. Other Employment
7. Professional Affiliations
8. Publications
9. Community Affiliations
10. Personal Data
11. References

All of these categories may not be relevant to your personal resume. From this list, however, you should be able to choose those which represent your background.

Writing a Resume

In putting the resume together there are several factors to keep in mind if you want the end result to be as effective as possible. Since this is your "first impression," make it a good one. Perhaps the following suggestions will help.

1. The items in each category should be in chronological order. They should be listed from the most recent to the most distant.
2. When listing degrees, arrange them so that the most advanced degree is mentioned first and work back as far as the high school degree.
3. Use subheads, written in all capitals, to separate each item you are including.
4. Parallel structure. Be sure that you follow through with a particular style throughout the resume. If you start listing your education by using dates, then use dates for every other category to start the item. If you start with a phrase in one section, use a similar phrase throughout.
5. Always date your resume in the upper right hand corner.
6. You will need to update the resume as you change your activities and add new dimensions to your career.
7. Always include references or an indication of where an interested party can contact references.
8. Make sure the resume is neat, legible, and clearly understandable.
9. Keep the resume as short as possible, avoiding all unnecessary and extraneous material.
10. Never include hobbies, interests, religious affiliation, or other trite comments.

SAMPLE RESUME

John Doe
111 Green Street
Hometown, U.S.A.
(742) 555-3456

November 1, 1980

Professional Objective
To obtain a managerial position in business with an emphasis on marketing/sales, particularly in computer sales.

Education
1975, M.B.A. Harvard University, Cambridge, Massachusetts
1972 Bachelor of Science, Economics, Brown University, cum laude, Providence, Rhode Island
1968 Graduate, Jonestown High School, Kansas City, Kansas

SAMPLE RESUME (Cont.)

Experience
1978–1980, Manager, computer sales, Price Computer Co., Greensville, Massachusetts
1976–1978, Assistant Manager Marketing/Sales, High Rock Computer Company, Microprocessors Division, Brownville, Illinois
1976–1977, Sales Representative, Computer Operations Inc., Boston, Massachusetts
1975–1976, Sales Representative, Transistor Recording Corp., New York City, New York
1973–1975, Part-time Sales Representative, Computer Operations Inc., Providence, Rhode Island

Professional Affiliations
1976–Present, Board of Directors and Member of Executive Board, National Organization of Sales Representatives
1978–Present, Member Computer Business Manager's Commission
1976–1979, Member Small Businessman's Association of Rhode Island

Community Affiliations
1978–Present, Member Hometown Industrial Commission
1976–1978, Member Hometown Planning Board
1977, Chairman Hometown Red Cross Drive

Personal Data
Married; Health: Excellent.

References
Can be obtained upon request by writing to Harvard University Placement Service, 1010 Massachusetts Avenue, Cambridge, Massachusetts 02717

SAMPLE RESUME DESIGNS

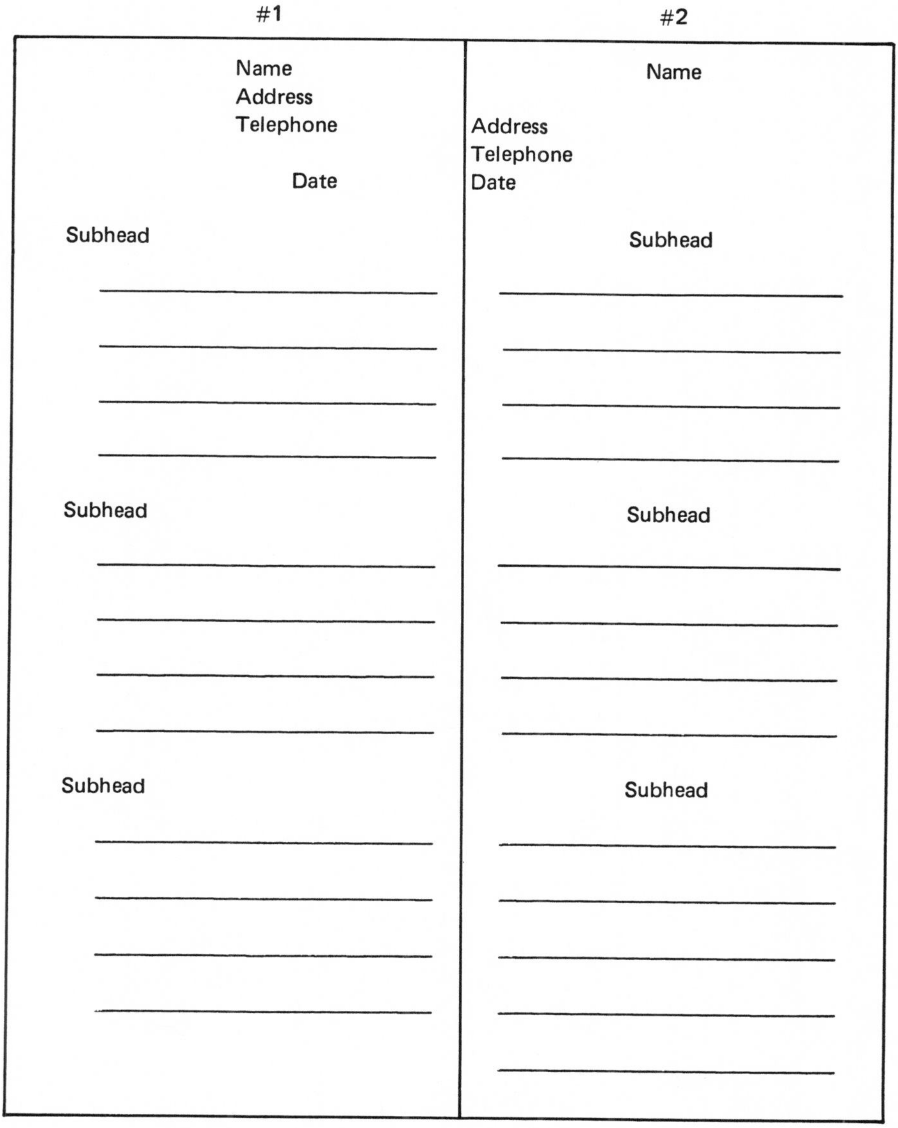

#1   #2

Name
Address
Telephone

Date

Subhead

_____

_____

_____

_____

Subhead

_____

_____

_____

_____

Subhead

_____

_____

_____

_____

Name

Address
Telephone
Date

Subhead

_____

_____

_____

_____

Subhead

_____

_____

_____

_____

Subhead

_____

_____

_____

_____